Grabbing a Spoon

Sheely Mauck

For my Mom and Appa

Thank you for your capacity to love unconditionally. I cannot imagine life without you, and I am eternally grateful for your love, trust, support, and friendship. From the beginning, I was yours, you were mine.

CONTENTS

Forward

To my readers:

As you will learn, it took me a long time to embark on this journey, and while I still have much to do and much to learn, I knew it was time to share my experiences with you. In the pages to follow, you will notice that stories will weave back and forth between different points of my life and "present" day through a series of tracks, including:

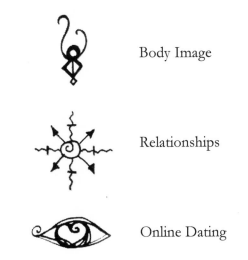

Body Image

Relationships

Online Dating

Towards the center of the book, I take you to my inner thoughts as I progressed through a relationship that had far more impact on my life than I prefer to admit – in short, he was the most significant love and tragic heartbreak of my young adult life.

Throughout, you will see references to songs, TV shows, and movies. Those close to me know that I have always had an eclectic taste in music and a love for connecting song lyrics to daily life. I have also drawn inspiration from the words of close friends, including those of Lorne, whose poem from many years ago helped frame the first story you will read in this book.

I have considered this book a work of autobiographical fiction. Wherever possible, I have kept the truth of the stories intact, changing only names and minor details to protect the privacy of individuals. For some stories, in which a change of names wouldn't be enough, I took creative license in developing new characters or narratives to share the intent and impact of particular interactions. Moreover, while I recount experiences with online dating, my intent is to share my stories rather than provide commentary on any particular dating site or strategy.

Before I conclude, there are two important friends to whom I must express my ultimate gratitude. Alisha and Tara:

Thank you for being my first ears on this "project" of mine and for creating the space for me to be more vulnerable and open with my heart than I have been with anyone before. I am honored to have had you join me from the beginning and am forever appreciative of your encouragement and willingness to hold me accountable and push me to dig deeper. Tara, beyond your editing skills, I believe your guidance and consultation have truly helped shape how I was able to tell my story. I am certain it is the better for it.

A Letter to Myself

December 2002

Dear Sheelarani,

You are just one month old, and you are so innocent and sweet. You do not have a care in the world, and you have your whole life ahead of you. But in a few months, you will get very sick and a disease called polio will paralyze you from the waist down. You are still so young and so beautiful, but you will never walk again. Do you know that your birth mother loves you more than the world itself? Do you know that she will make the ultimate sacrifice and give you up for adoption? You will cry, and you will not understand why your mother is leaving you…but one day, you will. Your mother wanted you to have all the opportunities that she could never have. She wanted you to succeed, and she believed you would do something great in the world. But she also knew that you would not survive in India, and that you needed medical attention that she could not afford to provide.

Sheelarani, would you believe me if I told you that you would be adopted by two wonderful people, half way around the world? Could you believe me if I said your adopted mother will love you more than all the stars in the sky? Would you believe me if I told you that you would never be able to imagine your life without her? You probably can't believe me, and that's okay. Just know that you are a survivor! You are filled with a magical spirit that will catch people by surprise, and slowly, you will change the world. You will come to know this, because this is what your adopted mother will tell you continuously throughout your life.

Sheely, if I told you the world was awesome would you believe me? Perhaps. Now you are 13, and you have been through so much. Your parents have already divorced, and both are remarried. You have spent more nights in a hospital in the last 7 years than most people will in their entire lifetime. But you have amazing friends, and you work hard in school. You have a wonderful, active social life and you are privileged to have inspiring leaders, coaches, and camp counselors who care about you. And never forget, your mom and dad will always love you.

Did you know that you are beautiful? Inside and out! Do you believe me? Sadly, you are already doubting your beauty. You have watched TV and

1

movies, and you look through teen magazines. You've seen the narrow-hipped, slender models, and you think to yourself that you look nothing like them. Sometimes you wonder what your biological mom looked like. Do you have her eyes, her mouth, her breasts? You will not get the answers you want. You carry on, holding the disappointment deep down inside you, and sometimes you stop eating even though you are still hungry.

How are you doing, Sheely? Things are pretty tough now. You are about to enter high school, and you are going to face so many obstacles. You are going to grow so much in four years, more than you ever have before. I'm sorry to say that you will have to deal with unfairness, prejudices, abused friends, drug overdoses, bomb threats, and school lockdowns. But, you will be strong and nothing will hold you back.

It's senior year! You now have to make life-changing decisions; everything will be going by so fast, and all you will want is for time to stop. You will frantically apply to colleges, cram for the SATs, and plan your senior prom. June comes, graduation passes. With a pounding, screaming heart, and the biggest smile you can manage, you will watch your best friend of 10 years board an airplane for an out-of-state school. Sobbing as you leave the airport, you will realize that your childhood has officially ended, and you will be on your way.

Did you know that you can be anyone you want to be? Did you know you can love who you want, do what you want, wear what you want, and love how you want? It will be hard to remember this, and if you forget sometimes, I will try my hardest to remind you. Do not let society tell you what you should be. You are your own woman, with your own personality, your own dreams, beliefs, wishes, and desires. Be sexy, be intelligent, be outspoken, be quiet when you want, and live life to the fullest. Be grateful for what you have, and remember that you are incredibly lucky. You have an education, a loving family, supportive friends, a roof over your head, a car to drive, and above all, freedom! Do not take your privileges for granted, and remember to think of those who are less fortunate. But do more than just think of them…work for them…help them…love them. You can make the world a better place, even it if is only one child at a time.

Sheely, remember that you are special and beautiful and unique. I know it is hard for you to believe everything I have said, but please try. I will continue to tell you with every bit of strength I have in my soul. I know there are many years to come and many questions yet to be answered. There are fears and uncertainties.

And all you want to know is if you will be successful. Well, in the words of Dr. Seuss, "Yes, you will indeed, 98 and ¾ percent guaranteed!"[1]

All my love,
Sheely

---

[1] Seuss, Dr. (1960). *Oh the Places You'll Go!*. New York: Random House, © 1990.

My Girls

During my days as a youth development professional, I would spend quite a bit of time working with teenagers, and at one point had a tight knit group of girls ranging between 7th and 10th grades. When they came in after school, their routine would include grabbing snack and then making their way to my office to hang out before starting their homework. These girls by far provided my fondest memories of working with youth.

Each one had a distinctive personality and they weren't afraid of asserting their differences in opinions or interests with each other. They each reminded me of how I was during that same time in my own life, and while they exuded confidence in many regards, I could see the subtle insecurities they each held, but did their best to cover up. Our conversations were wide and varied and covered such territory as school, teachers, and upcoming dances, and would often venture into social justice and relationships. Of course, discussing relationships was their top favorite.

Teens always want to know all about you and your world outside of the program. Younger kids rarely care about such details, but teens want to be "in the know," and will even make up details of your life, including who you're dating. We would spend hours talking about boys; boys they liked, boys they didn't like, boys they might like, boys someone else should like. And surely they couldn't leave out a most intriguing topic – boys I should like. They were convinced I was involved with the technology director, and if I wasn't, then I should be. If not him, then undoubtedly I was with the operations director. If they believed that I was in fact single, then the conversation switched gears. They had a problem to solve!

"Sheely, you should join *eHarmony*!" Amy would say.

"No, she should try *ChristianMingle.com* – my sister met her boyfriend there!" added Alyssa.

"Sheely – smile!" they'd command as they snapped photos of me on their phones. "Oh, that one will make a perfect profile picture!" They loved to joke about setting up an account for me.

In part to play along, I would dramatically tell them not to do so, but thinking back, I was equally split. Part of me was curious about online dating – could it actually work? Could I actually find someone that I would like? The other part was so self-conscious about whether I, a person using a wheelchair and a bit chubby, would even be attractive to someone online. I couldn't articulate out loud all the concerns in my own head, but I had elaborate back and forth conversations with myself while thinking that the girls just couldn't understand the logistics of *me* doing online dating. How do you explain who you are, how you live, and how you negotiate through life in a profile? How can you come close to explaining your life to a stranger enough to attract them to respond? It all seemed too complex, too risky, and highly unlikely to be successful.

How would I present myself? What photos would I use? Is it safe? Where would I meet them and be able to arrive and navigate on my own? All of these questions, doubts, and glimmers of hope and curiosity swirled around in my head every time the girls brought the subject up. It was a jumbled up mess of thoughts, self-doubt, and low self-esteem.

It was in these moments that I was overcome with hypocrisy and a twinge of shame. I have always stood firmly and proudly on being an honest and open youth development professional. While recognizing that "teens will be teens", I was still going to set a positive example for them, including being conscientious about sharing what I liked. I knew that my opinions and choices reflected the young woman I hoped they would aspire to be. Music is of course a common interest and an easy way to relate to teens. I was always careful to express my personal liking of songs that had appropriate lyrics, and not necessarily just songs without swearing, but rather I wanted to make sure I endorsed songs or movies that represented women, relationships, and careers in a positive and healthy light. If there was a song that I happened to like that didn't do this, and the teens ranted about how great it was, I would use the opportunity to show how the lyrics sent the wrong message. It wasn't that I thought they would fall for it every time, but it seemed to me that if I was consistent enough on the subject, eventually they might get a nugget of what I was trying to teach them.

Music and media can be such powerful teachers in a teen's life, that I took it upon myself to talk about it, to pay attention to the innuendos, to hopefully inspire them to open their eyes, ears, and opinions too. Constant, consistent messaging has to get in there eventually, I hoped. I wanted to model that it was okay to listen intently to music or to watch your favorite shows, but to recognize when media is stereotyping or manipulating reality into false truths. This is still important to me, and something I really wanted my girls to at least understand, if not be motivated by it too. I also wanted my girls to always be aware of their true beauty and that the most beautiful version of you is when you're being your true, authentic self.

Yet, as the girls encouraged me to try online dating, my deep down resistance was that I felt like I wasn't pretty enough or good enough or worthy enough for anyone to find me attractive from a simple online profile. I couldn't share these insecurities with them, so instead I deflected the issue or made light of the conversation by laughing off their gestures and assuring them it was never going to happen in an overly dramatized way, which always resulted in chuckles. I didn't want them to know the truth. If I had ever let on to my misgivings they would never trust me again. How could I be trusted with their insecurities and doubts, their dreams and goals, if I wasn't able to model what I was teaching them? It would be a devastating blow to them if they knew what was rustling around in my heart and my head. Why should they believe me when I say it's your true self that really matters when clearly I wasn't able to fully subscribe to the same belief in my own life? As a youth development professional, I always avoided falling into the cliché pocket of "do as I say, not as I do." I had made a conscious choice in my career to lead from the floor, to live the life I was advocating for them, to be real, true, and honest. Yet here I was being less than genuine and authentic with my girls whom I so adored.

In many ways, I wish I could have another afternoon with them. I'd like to collect them all in my old office and have another chance, another conversation, another opportunity to be honest with them. If I close my eyes, I can still picture my girls – three or four of them squished on to the green couch, another sitting in the spare office chair, two more sitting with legs criss-crossed on the floor and their homework sprawled out in front of them. I can hear their raucous laughter and multiple threads of conversations occurring simultaneously. Looking back at those days and reflecting on where I am now, I've realized how much I've grown and changed. I have finally come to a place where I feel confident and comfortable in my skin. Yes, I still have some insecurities and aspects about my body that I don't like, but I no longer wonder if someone can, or wants to love me as I am. Now it's a matter of finding the right person that fits with who I am in this moment.

To thine own self be true. And when your girls think you float on air, make sure that you're not blowing hot air in their direction. If I could do it all over again, I'd say it. Out loud. "I'm afraid of online dating, because what if someone can't decipher my profile and see me for who I am? What if no one responds? What if it all goes terribly wrong?" And they would roar at the top of their teenage lungs and all at once they'd shriek "Sheely, you are crazy! You're amazing! And smart! You're the smartest person we know! Of course someone will fall madly in love with you! And we HAVE to meet him and approve of him! Because, Sheely, you are so valuable to us that just any old guy won't do. You need someone as amazing as you are."

Venturing in

I had finally created a plan. I was going to start online dating *next* summer. I had numerous reasons for delaying this most dreaded task. I suppose more like rationalizations as to why waiting until next summer was the way to go. Probably, in all fairness, it was easier to think about online dating if I put off the actual start date, if I stalled the reality of it. If it was still just something I could talk about, not something with which I would actually go through, it was better. If it was future tense, I wouldn't have to know what the outcome might be or not be. I wouldn't have to acknowledge my feelings of inadequacy or doubt. I was merely preparing and planning for potential change. I was just beginning to be willing to entertain the idea of meeting someone. In thinking of Dr. Prochaska's *Stages of Change*, I was definitely just on the cusp of the contemplation phase – nowhere near action.

I happened to mention my plan to my friend Madeline over dinner. She listened and then with a slight smile, asked, "What about right now? You said work has been pretty quiet lately."

I wasn't exactly sure how to answer, but I explained that I wanted more time to get to a weight that I felt happy with. Right now was too soon. Spring was my absolute busiest time of the year for business, so that led to the reasonable conclusion that *next* summer would be the perfect time.

"Plus, I don't want to pay for service yet, and I don't want a site that's just about hook ups. When I actually do this, I was thinking of a site like eHarmony, you know – something…more serious," I managed to explain.

"You could try *OkCupid!*, it's free," she responded with that gleam in her eye that meant she was going to win this one. We had been friends long enough that I knew when her logic was going to beat out my logic. We were a fair match for sure, but she had a way of looking me in the eye, recognizing when I was stalling or feeling vulnerable, and then moving in for the motivational push out of my comfort zone. I knew that once she shoved me off my balance she would be by my side through the entire adventure, regardless of the outcome. I knew she was right.

I stayed silent for a minute, sipped again from my glass, scrambled my brain for another good reason to not start, and slowly exhaled.

Madeline broke the silence, "I just don't think you should keep such a long timeline. There's too much room for talking yourself out of it. Think of this as practice. Try it for free, then next summer you can think about eHarmony. I'll help you write your profile and everything. It really isn't as scary as you're making it out to be. You have total control over who you talk to and who you don't. You can do this. I promise."

While I wasn't entirely convinced to jump in when I left her house after dinner, her message must have sunk in. I came home, poured a glass of water, and Googled *okcupid.com*.

I took a deep breath, ignored my uneasy stomach, and slowly started to dig in. The less I engaged my rational brain, the easier it was. If I just kept going through the motions, following the questions down the rabbit hole, then I wouldn't talk myself out of what I was doing.

Answering the initial round of questions was easy, and I'll admit, even a little fun. Then came time for writing the actual profile; I could barely keep my brain from screaming at me to stop. What was I going to write for the self-summary? How do I summarize myself in a witty, interesting, captivating, or even just a not-too-boring way?

Do I immediately mention that I use a wheelchair? Should I be direct, offer a subtle implication, or not write anything and let the photos do the talking? Oh great, now I have to pick a photo! I wanted a cute one, but I also felt the need to show the full me – me, in my chair. I settled for a cropped Facebook profile picture – me with sunglasses and a cute black dress with just a touch of cleavage showing and a second, slightly blurry photo taken of me just before going to a holiday party. The holiday photo revealed me in my favorite red dress with a beautiful broach my mom made just for that dress, and of course, my ever-constant accessory of a chair.

There was one profile question about the most private fact you'd be willing to share. I initially thought I would somehow use the space to share that I had total feeling from head to toe and full control of my body, or something to that effect. I was thinking that with dating relationships, the issue of sex needed to be addressed. I wanted to get the issue out of the way – I wanted potential interested matches to know that I had sensory feeling; polio was not like other common forms of paralysis. I can feel, control my bodily functions (yeah, that sounds sexy) and mostly, I can and do enjoy sex. How do you convey that without a) seeming like you just want to hook up, b) sounding like a medical professional or c) some combination of a) and b) with a hint of arrogance?

After half an hour or so, I had an answer posted that was a mix of a) and c), but came to the conclusion that I didn't feel comfortable broaching this subject on my front page profile. I knew it would be important, but it just seemed *too* personal at this point. Besides, I wasn't even going to start this for another year, and here I was at the crossroads of to reveal or not to reveal. I opted for a less intimate fact: that I love to dance, but will only do so if encouraged by those around me. I thought that was daring enough for me at this point. Since I felt like I needed a bridge, I also offered up that I would answer more specific questions if asked. I may be shy virtually, but I am honest and straightforward in person.

I spent another hour or so answering profile questions. "Would you date someone who is messy?" "Do you like to discuss or debate politics?" "Star Wars or Star Trek?"

Finally, just after 12:30 in the morning, I hit the 200 mark. I saw that some people had answered over 500 questions, but my mind was pretty much at its end, and so was the glass of wine I had poured around question number 43. Now it was time for bed. I glanced over the profile once more, then signed out. There was nothing to do now, but wait and see.

The first things people usually notice about me:

To be honest, most people will first notice that I use a wheelchair. The next - I have a great smile and am very comfortable in my own skin. Of course, if I'm wearing a low-cut top, my cleavage might be the first thing people notice.

Humpty Dumpty's Scars

When I was young, my mom would read Mother Goose nursery rhymes to me every night. I loved hearing about *Mary, Mary Quite Contrary*, eating her curds and whey or *Peter, Peter, Pumpkin Eater*. *Humpty Dumpty* was always one of my favorites. Humpty Dumpty was an egg:

Humpty Dumpty sat on a wall
Humpty Dumpty had a big fall
All of the king's horses and all of the king's men
Couldn't put Humpty Dumpty back together again

I'm not sure at what point I started to use *Humpty Dumpty* as an analogy for the consequences of my childhood surgeries, but it was probably during middle school when the first insecurities about how I looked began to emerge. I spent many childhood days at a children's hospital in Portland. Prior to going into kindergarten I had corrective surgeries on both hips, knees, and ankles. The six surgeries were completed in one single shot, since the idea was to get everything completed as quickly as possible instead of dragging it out through individual surgeries. A younger child can heal faster than an older child, so if all the corrections were made at the same time, the theory was that I would heal quicker and more completely than if they dragged them out over a few years.

I don't remember the surgery being traumatizing, or the restrictions of the full body cast being insufferable. I was young enough and healthy enough to handle the impact of the surgeries and heal. Ultimately, the surgeries allowed me to utilize leg braces so I could stand and walk with the assistance of crutches. The incisions healed and my joints seemed to work well enough.

The summer before 4th grade, I underwent additional surgeries on my knees and ankles to release and correct some contractures that had developed over the years. I had become accustomed to the trips to the hospital, even though they made me anxious. I knew they were for my benefit, but at the time, they made me even more different than the other kids at school.

We started to notice some issues after the original surgeries, and then more after the 4th grade surgery. By middle school, I began to realize that while the doctors had essentially taken me apart, they hadn't put me back together correctly. As I grew up, the distortions became more noticeable. Instead of my ankles turning outward, the doctors had overcompensated and turned them too far inward.

This was also the era in which I inherited a windswept leg. When you follow my legs from my hips to my ankles, you'll notice that my left leg takes a 30 degree turn below the knee. It's as if a severe wind blew in from the west and bowed my left leg with its force. This differential created an inch or so disparity in length between my legs. We would learn later that the gravity of this differentiation would also exacerbate the scoliosis that riddled my spine. The scoliosis became so severe that I ended up having the longest surgery of my life during 7th grade. Twelve hours of surgery and 11 days of recovery later, I grew four inches and had plenty of scars to show for it. I missed so much school that year, I ended up enrolling in home school, though I managed to keep in close contact with friends by spending some afternoons each week attending after-school programs.

Prior to the back surgery, my hips had the most obvious and unappealing scars. It never bothered me too much, but as I got older, I began to detest them and the asymmetry of my legs. Aside from my left leg being windswept, even my hips didn't seem to be attached correctly. The left side seemed to flow naturally like anyone else's leg, but my right hip looked as if the doctors had rotated my leg ever so slightly, so that there was an extra few inches between the hip socket and where my thigh started. It's more likely that the doctors didn't make their incisions in the same place on both hips, so when they sewed me back up, I was no longer aligned. From a medical perspective I really don't know what happened, even though we have our medical scrapbook of files and documents somewhere in our family treasures. Nevertheless, the bottom line is that after all the surgeries, incisions, doctor visits, missed school, physical therapy and body casts, my legs were officially, awkwardly, and forever asymmetrical.

The scars from my back surgery had equal issues. The fortunate difference is that I can't see the long scar down my spine; and of all the scars it's probably the nicest. Thin, smooth, and straight. The one that I abhor starts midway on the right side of my back and runs around my torso halfway across the front of my abdomen, following the cadence of my rib cage. Although the scar is soft and you can hardly feel it, the front looks like a weird, twisted smile. To date I have refused to ever show my stomach in public to anyone. Up until recently it was easy to hide and wasn't a big deal because I also didn't like the size of my tummy, so two-piece swimsuits were always out.

However, since making a commitment a couple years ago to lose weight and live a healthier lifestyle, more recently I have begun to consider wearing a bikini. Yet, no matter how thin I get, the scar will always be there. I go back to the age-old question that rattles around in my head: will I ever truly feel comfortable in my skin? Will I ever be able to look past the scars and the asymmetry of my body?

Even if all the king's horses and all the king's men were successful in putting Humpty Dumpty back together again, could he be truly whole?

Perhaps.

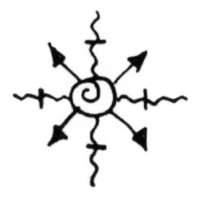

A Boyfriend for a Day

When I was little, I had many boyfriends. Beginning in preschool through 2nd grade there were boys that I liked, and boys that I didn't. Like any girl my age, I was exploring my tastes and opinions, which no doubt changed from day to day. I was constantly interested in someone, and for the most part, the boys reciprocated feelings and liked me back. I was getting pretty good at knowing what I liked, including the triplets. I'm certain all three were my boyfriend at some point however briefly, but Jackson was always my favorite.

As we got older and the boys started noticing the pretty girls, my relationships began to dwindle. Although there was a boy I liked very much in 5th grade. We both played the saxophone in band and we had a bit of a friendly competition going about who was going to retain the 1st chair position. I knew Chris had a crush on Sally, but he always talked with me and we seemed to have fun together.

It was a long time ago, and memories can evolve and turn into stories with more or less of their details intact. In my story, I remember Chris asking me one day if I wanted to be his girlfriend. I was ecstatic! I went home after school that day feeling on top of the world, like I had never felt before. The rapture of being asked out was almost too much to contain. I couldn't wait to go back to school the next day. Even better, it was band day which meant we went to school early for practice.

Sadly, the drama began to unfold in slow motion, right before my eyes. Some of the other kids already knew, but unbeknownst to me Sally had been playing hard to get and had already told Chris that she didn't want to be his girlfriend. Apparently, that was when he turned and asked me. His motive had been to make her jealous. It totally worked. By the time I got to school, even though it was early for band practice, Chris had already decided to dump me. His plan had been so successful that he and Sally were already boyfriend and girlfriend.

Writing about this now, I realize the triviality of it. As a pre-teen exploring the world of dating for the very first time, I remember the feelings of devastation and heartbreak crash through the cloud of euphoria. For a long time I would wonder what Sally had that I didn't. It was one of the few times in my life I can remember being truly envious of someone else's ability to run out on the grass or climb the jungle gym or play basketball like she and Chris did. I know, because I watched them during recess from the hard top of the playground.

I can still remember waiting for my mom to pick me up after school on that most disappointing of days. The sun was shining, and it was one of the first warm spring days we had had in a long while. I saw Sally off to my left, walking across the grass with a friend. They stopped and faced each other. She placed one hand on her hip as she brushed her perfect blonde hair away from her face with the other. She was wearing a cute skirt with sandals. As I watched her, I knew she was having just one of countless experiences that I would never have: standing in the middle of the grass on a beautiful, spring day, walking home after school with her friend, and yes, being the girlfriend of the boy I so very much liked. None of these experiences would ever be mine.

I looked away, turning my gaze to the right, then glanced back toward the parking lot. There was mom, ready to lift me into the car, so we could go home. I pushed the thoughts of Sally and Chris down, deep down, where I put all the thoughts that were not to be shared with anyone. I breathed in and exhaled slowly. Done. The thoughts were gone. It was over for now. It was time to forget and move on as best I could.

"How was your day, sweetheart?" My mom asked me this every day, and always with a smile.

I smiled back and gave my most common response to her daily question, "It was fine. How was yours?"

Breaking the Ice

It was a day after posting my profile that I had my first message on *OkCupid!* All it said was, "Love."

I reluctantly decided to check out his profile. I hated knowing that each person I visited would see that I had viewed their profile – but I definitely didn't want to pay for the upgraded account that allowed you to view profiles anonymously. This guy seemed pretty nice though. Tall and a bit on the heavy side, but with a cute smile. According to the site statistics, we had a fairly high compatibility rate (86%), we shared similar religious and political beliefs, and in his personal summary he mentioned how he believed each of us has talents and characteristics that make us beautiful in our own ways. He was looking for a woman who was comfortable in her own skin.

So, I hit the reply button, and stared at the blank message screen. What to say? After all, he had only written a single word. I would start typing…"Hi, how are you?" and then hit the delete button.

Finally, I forced myself to just write what came to mind without deleting words until after I had at least a couple sentences. After a good half hour, I eventually settled on, "Thanks for the message. I enjoyed reading your profile. Feel free to write back, ask a question, or tell me something more about yourself." I took a shallow breath and held it. Then I hit send.

Whew! Thank God that was over!

He wrote back the next day, and what had been an underlying concern for me was brought to the surface in his response. After acknowledging that he didn't know if it was appropriate, he asked how I ended up using a chair and said he'd always be wondering if he didn't ask. In some ways, I was glad he brought it up. The door had been opened for me to address the elephant in the room without having to bring it up myself.

"No problem at all," I wrote. "I always appreciate people who are willing to ask what's on their mind. If I don't feel comfortable answering a question, I'll say so. I was born in India, and did not get vaccinated right away, so contracted polio when I was 7 months old. I was adopted just before turning 4 and I've lived in the Northwest ever since. Polio is less known about these days, but a key difference between me and others who use chairs is that I have total feeling from head to toe (something I am absolutely grateful for!). The only thing the polio did was damage the nerves to my actual leg muscles, and it weakened my right arm just a bit."

I then transitioned to asking about his work and some projects he was working on.

His response couldn't have been more perfect.

He was familiar with polio from his grandfather who had minor paralysis in one leg and he emphasized that it was great I had feeling and didn't mind questions since he was "insatiably curious."

So far, this whole online dating thing seemed to be going okay. I liked this guy. He was articulate, thoughtful and seemed genuine. Emailing seemed fairly harmless.

All was going well…until I received a message from a new guy asking if I wanted to meet up for drinks or coffee. I panicked for a moment - okay, more like 15 minutes as I just stared at the message speechless. He hadn't asked me about using a chair or anything else about who I was, and yet he was ready to meet? Had he even reviewed my profile? He must have, right? The inner dialogue in my head went on for another 10 minutes or so before I could get myself to the point of being capable of writing a response.

I liked my standard intro of "Thanks for the message," so I started with that. I then shared that I was new to the online world and wasn't yet sure about meeting in person. I clicked "send," took another deep breath, and called it a night.

He wrote back the next morning saying he wasn't looking for anything romantic, but understood and said "maybe next time." He was going to be in Seattle for a conference, another reason that pushed my reluctance button. By the sound of it, he seemed to be looking for hook ups while he was traveling. Maybe he was. I don't know, but I certainly wasn't going to meet him.

To my surprise, in came another new message asking how it was going and if I'd like to get a coffee or a beer and chat. I looked at this new guy's profile, and he actually seemed pretty cute and he had a decently completed profile. Unlike the guy visiting from out of town for a day, this one lived and worked here, so I wrote a short message – "Hi, yeah, I'd be up for talking over coffee." I hovered over the send button, wondering in my head, "What if he says okay? What if I have to figure out a place for us to meet?" I had given some thought to these steps in my head, but to actually execute them was a whole different ball game. Instead of "Send," I clicked "Save Draft."

Meanwhile, I hadn't heard from the first guy with the grandfather who had polio. I was actually interested in meeting him – I was excited to meet him in fact – logistics aside, yet he seemed to have disappeared. I liked that we were writing back and forth. We were getting to know each other. He had shared personal facts and so had I. To be fair, I'm sure I also liked the fact that he was going through a divorce and wasn't 100% looking for a new relationship, at least not yet. Starting off as friends seemed much more appealing and *much easier* to meet for a "date." It would be low-stakes, low-risk, and safe.

I continued to hold off on agreeing to meet anyone, but the pressure to "connect" was increasing.

"Oh crap! Now this guy wants to talk on the phone or text?!" I said to Madeline over the phone. She had called me within hours of receiving my text saying I was definitely on a roll and getting messages from new guys almost every day. The latest one, Peter, worked with youth and grew up not too far from me – he went to the neighboring high school and graduated just a couple years ahead. We did seem to have quite a bit in common, but he wanted my number? Really?

I feel silly admitting this, but I actually Googled how to block a person's number from your cell phone. I have had my mobile number since I was 18 and I didn't want to get rid of it, but I worried about what to do if I gave my number to Peter. What would I do if he kept calling and I no longer wanted him to be able to reach me? I wouldn't give my work number because really, I preferred to start with text messages before actually talking on the phone.

He sent a couple other messages with different questions. I answered those and conveniently ignored the one about talking on the phone. I started to write an answer with my number. I deleted it. I started again, then paused. I eventually realized that for him to text me, he'd have to give me his number too. This required trust on both ends. I finally wrote, "Here's my number. I'd prefer to text as I tend to multi-task in the evenings, so I'm not the best conversationalist."

Half an hour later, I heard my phone buzz, alerting me of a new text. It was Peter, and to my great relief, it wasn't the end of the world. Initially, we answered some basic questions again about our interests.

Then he asked, "Do you have any photos?" At first, I thought it was more of a suggestive request. I didn't want to go *there*.

"I only have the photos already on OKC on my phone right now."

"Oh, ok." He then sent me a very classic mirror reflection shot…shirtless, serious face. I'd be lying if I said I didn't enjoy the photo. He was *quite* nice looking. I still didn't send him one.

The next day, I had a "Good morning – hope you have a wonderful day" message waiting for me, which I must admit put a smile on my face. There was still the issue though of meeting someone in person.

I opened my previously saved draft for the prospective coffee/beer date, and hit send. He wrote back right away suggesting Friday night. I honestly did have other plans scheduled, and yes, I was absolutely relieved of this fact. So I told him I already had plans that I couldn't break and asked him in what area of Seattle he lived.

"Bothell."

I had no response to give. It was almost a deer in the headlights moment.

I couldn't believe he was in frickin' Bothell. When people say they are from a city in their profile, you assume they actually live in that city. To this day, I don't know any places in Bothell that I'd be comfortable enough to choose as a rendezvous. Who goes to Bothell anyway? It's a town northeast of downtown Seattle and in the complete opposite direction of where I lived. It takes forever to get there with traffic. It's an eastside suburb in my eyes. But what did I know? I had never been there before and certainly couldn't navigate my way there without a GPS.

The concept of meeting strangers was a sizeable deterrent for me when I was going through the stages of contemplating the whole online dating thing. While my car gives me tremendous flexibility and freedom, it has its limitations as well. There are rarely enough parking spaces with sufficiently wide cross hatches for the lift. Sometimes, even if there is accessible parking, it isn't close enough to the entrance of the building. I still have to wheel myself across roadways and crosswalks. I avoid doing this alone since I sit so low to the ground and can't exactly sprint out of the way should an oncoming car not see me. Perhaps I'm too cautious. Perhaps I am just cautious enough. When meeting up with friends or family, it is routine for them to drive with me, meet me at my car, or move my car if I have to double park so I have enough room to use the lift. Then we all cross the road together, with their eyes high enough to see above the hoods of parked cars and monitor oncoming traffic.

However, meeting someone that I've only met online is not the same as meeting up with a friend. I want to be able to arrive and leave independently without the need of anyone's assistance. What if I don't like the person? What if he turns out to not be who he said he was? I don't want to be dependent on anyone anyway, much less be in a situation like this. Finding places that fit my criteria can be challenging. Unfortunately, such places tend to be more commercialized locations like chain restaurants and malls. The Cheesecake Factory downtown has a garage just behind it that I've parked in several times. South Center Mall and Pacific Place Mall are good too. There is one coffee shop operated by a nonprofit that is a great location, but it's only open weekdays from 9am to 3pm, which ironically are not ideal times for dates. These were my "safe zones." I wasn't ready to venture outside of those, though I did expand my list of places to include a dim sum restaurant that happens to have a huge parking garage.

After another week or so, I suggested dim sum to Zach, another guy that started emailing me while I delayed responding to Mr. Bothel. Zach had been emailing me twice a day, while Peter (the shirtless selfie guy) just kept sending the same three text messages: How are you? Hope you're having a great day. How's it going? It was getting old and I was bitterly annoyed.

I still couldn't bring myself to share my exact reason for choosing the dim sum place, but I said they had free, easy parking. Zach seemed really nice and perceptive. When he asked about wanting to meet, he qualified the question by saying he suspected I would want to correspond more before meeting in person based on some of the responses to questions I had answered. Essentially, he knew I was hesitant about meeting face to face, and I felt like I had been given a bit of "an out" when it came to suggesting specific places. Plus, from his personality questions, I knew he wouldn't mind if I ran a Google search, so I felt free to ask for his last name and I conducted a bit of research ahead of time.

This was how I liked to proceed with both academic endeavors and when faced with the unfamiliar – methodically and systematically research what I can in order to draw reasonable conclusions or recommendations for how to move forward. So, I ran the search. His artistic work came up right away, and the personal bio on his website intrigued me even more.

"Okay," I said out loud. "I think I can do this."

I opened the message thread and wrote: "Hi Zach, how about dim sum this Sunday at 11:30?"

As I briefly hovered over the "send" button, my seemingly favorite position in this new venture, I swiftly shook my head side to side, took a deep breath, and whispered, "here goes."

"I believe most things in life exist on continuums, especially when it comes to personalities. We are complex creatures in a complex world, and rarely can you boil any one issue (or person) down to 140 characters or less without omitting pertinent details. If you ask me yes/no or other dichotomous questions, I might answer, but I will try to qualify the answer with the exceptions, though I have some definitive interests, tastes, and preferences."

George Gray

I have studied many times
The marble which was chiseled for me –
A boat with a furled sale at rest in a harbor.
In truth it pictures not my destination
But my life.
For love was offered me and I shrank from its
disillusionment;
Sorrow knocked at my door, but I was afraid;
Ambition called to me, but I dreaded the chances.
Yet all the while I hungered for meaning in my life.
And now I know that we must lift the sail
And catch the winds of destiny
Wherever they drive the boat.
To put meaning in one's life may end in madness,
But life without meaning is the torture
Of restlessness and vague desire –
It is a boat longing for the sea and yet afraid.

By: Edgar Lee Masters

Funny Thighs

We were fortunate that the hospital in Portland was willing to accept me as a patient. Since they scholarship their services and my numerous corrective leg and back surgeries consumed my childhood, we were truly lucky for the care and resources they provided. I can say this now, as an adult. As a child, I was not appreciative of this fact. I hated the hospital. I used to get sick to my stomach driving down to Portland. We did it so many times that as soon as we passed the final rest stop, before driving over the big green bridge, it would take all my concentration to not throw-up.

I never told anyone this when I was young. I kept it to myself. I knew it was for my own good, and I didn't want to make my mom worry. I would swallow my own secret on each trip. Swallow the sick feeling. Swallow the fear of another surgery. Swallow the pain. Swallow the pain I knew my parents went through each time. I still get a little sick to my stomach if I have to drive directly into Portland. I prefer to take I-205 and come at the city from the east, or in many ways I try to avoid Portland all together. God forbid I have to cross the Beaverton Bridge or go anywhere near The Hill.

Of all the surgeries, all the doctor visits, all the follow up exams, I vaguely remember one conversation in particular with my primary doctor. I was used to him and the other doctors and physical therapists giving me all sorts of instructions and warnings about following directions and if I didn't, then untold things would happen and I would be much worse off. This time, he was warning me about puberty and the changes that would happen. I believe the point of the conversation was that I needed to stay active. I needed to keep swimming, standing, and walking in the leg braces I was still using. The leg braces would prove to be terribly impractical as I grew older, especially when puberty hit, but at this point, I was still an active kid. I could get around as well as my friends and was a pretty normal fourth grader, all things considered.

He was telling me that as my body started to change, my weight would distribute in certain ways and I would likely have a lot of weight on my thighs. He was trying to be direct and gentle, saying things without hurting my feelings. Like most adults, he was planting a seed that he hoped I would one day remember and understand. Call it knowledge, call it inevitable, call it what you want. I was jinxed and forever condemned to have big thighs from that moment forward. This is what my brain registered, held on to, and immortalized. It was this statement that made puberty even more difficult for me, making my teen years and any sense of self-esteem a struggle. I was cursed with big thighs.

I hadn't given the doctor much thought in that moment. It wasn't like I was traumatized at hearing his warning. Instead, it was a slow seeping poison that I began to believe on a visceral level. After all, I was used to hearing doctors' orders and their typical warnings. They were the adults. They always knew better or knew best. Because I was quiet and well-behaved, it was easy to overlook that I was also quite stubborn. I would often forgo their rehab exercises, the stretching, or other post-op instructions. I thought they were a nuisance. When I would show up for any of the numerous follow up visits and they knew I hadn't followed their instructions in between visits, it made me dislike them even more. How had they *known*? I was incredulous that they were omniscient and knew what I had or hadn't done.

A few years later, when I was 12, I had decided that I definitely liked one of my guy friends. We had established a love-hate relationship, like most pre-pubescent relationships. I remember sitting with him and a couple of our friends. It was summer, and I was wearing stretchy spandex shorts because they were the easiest to wear. I hadn't reached a level of fashion awareness yet; that would come in the next few years. I was still a kid wearing practical clothes for my body.

In our carefree conversations, we were all chattering and talking. Laughing and hanging out. I don't remember how his comment had been preceded, how we were on the subject, or how he decided to say what he said. It was a casual comment, not meant to harm, not meant to make fun of, just something that came out of his mouth and into my heart.

"Your thighs look funny," was all he said.

As most childhood memories, I don't know what I said in response, if anything at all. We probably continued on chattering and laughing about everything and anything. What hurt the most is that he was right. He and that damn doctor were both right. Here I was just 12 years old and already I had big funny looking thighs.

The emotionally balanced explanation is that since I have no muscle strength in my legs, my calves are very slender; I can almost close my thumb and index finger around my ankles. However, puberty had kicked in and sure enough the doctor's *curse* came true. I had gained weight and it decided to distribute around my thighs, only there were no muscles in my upper legs either. The result is really flat, wide thighs with no shape. From my knees, my legs taper rapidly down to my petite feet. Imagine the thighs of a slightly overweight teenage girl connected to the lower legs of a very malnourished 10-year-old girl. That was me in all my funny thighs glory.

From the moment of his comment on, when I was in my chair I began to cross my legs. By crossing, I believed my thighs took on a natural shape and the dramatic tapering wasn't as obvious. To this day, I will not go in public with my legs uncrossed and in plain sight. If I am carrying a big box or something else on my lap to cover my thighs, then I will keep them uncrossed. As soon as my lap is free, I lift my left leg over my right and tuck them into their feminine posture. When I am around close friends and family I am less self-conscious and don't always cross. However, I promise that if I can help it, you will never find me in public being anything less than a proper lady with her legs gracefully crossed.

Recently, I hurt my right leg and couldn't stand to have any weight on top of it, so I learned how to navigate crossing my right leg over my left. It was a bit of an adjustment, especially since I was so experienced at balancing objects like dinner plates, books, or my purse on my lap when my legs were crossed the other way. You wouldn't think it would make much of a difference, but my lap took a surprisingly different shape when crossing my right leg over my left. The overall goal was nonetheless achieved – diminish the appearance of those funny thighs.

As I write about this childhood intersection now, I know it's silly. I know that if my friend knew his words had such a deep impact on me, he would feel terrible. It was one of the first instances I remember where I knew I really didn't, and would probably never, fit the common image of beauty in our society. Call this my coming of age or my first adult awareness in my youthful consciousness, but back then I didn't know how to articulate this realization. Like so many examples of moments that shaped my definition of me, I never spoke about it with anyone. Instead, I found the best solutions I could. Not only did I start crossing my legs, I also started taking a fanny pack, and eventually a purse, with me everywhere I went. It would sit on my lap and fill up, or cover up, some of the space created by my wide thighs. My mom and some friends would joke with me about needing my security blanket, but I still never discussed my feelings or thoughts behind it. I never explained that I was insecure with the size of my legs or the shape of my body.

From that day forward, I also stopped wearing fitted shorts and opted for longer ones that went to my knees. Eventually, I stopped wearing shorts all together. I learned not to look at my thighs. During freshman year of high school, when I had to swim, I would sit and cover up with a towel while keeping both legs criss-crossed when I sat on the side of the pool waiting to get in or out. I put away all pictures that showed me with my funny thighs. I knew I could never change them, so I stopped looking. I hid, denied, ignored the funny, disgusting, disfigured, abnormal pieces of me. Or so I believed.

I thought that by ignoring them, they would no longer have control over how I felt. They couldn't make me unhappy, self-conscious, or sad. As I grew up, I realized that there was nothing I could do. They would always be a part of me. They would always be what I see when I look down. They support me. They help me sit in my chair. They are my foundation most of the day. They are my funny thighs. They are me - just a part of me I don't like and don't like others to fully see. But they are mine.

Dim Sum Date

I had never really been in the dating scene until I started the online dating experiment. The whole concept of meeting and getting to know someone you haven't worked with, known through school, or through family and friends was foreign to me.

I can recall only one other instance when I went out for a meal with someone I had just met and had no other common connection with. I was working for a youth agency in South Seattle and we had a group of volunteers from out of state visiting for the day. He was one of the coordinators and after talking with him for a while during a break, he asked if I wanted to join him for dinner that evening. I agreed. I was excited and exhilarated and scared at the same time because I had *never* done this before. He was older, my guess was about 15 years older, but he was interesting and I didn't really think of it as a date because he didn't live here and thus there was no prospect of a relationship. Regardless, I told my co-worker where I was going just to be safe and I picked the Cheesecake Factory as the location with its fabulous parking garage and easy navigation. This occurred over 6 years ago now, so the dim sum date definitely felt like a brand new experience. Plus, there were some added stakes – there could be potential for something more.

I was definitely feeling a little nervous about meeting Zach. I wasn't sure what to expect, and as I'm sure many do, I debated between multiple outfits: a dress, the skirt and blouse combo, or dressy pants and blouse. At last, I chose a black cotton dress with ¾ length sleeves and a white embroidered design down the front. He sent me a text in the morning to confirm. There was no going back.

I put on my favorite turquoise earrings and opted for just a little mascara instead of full on eyeliner and eye shadow. I go through phases of wearing makeup every day, and this was definitely not one of those phases. Plus, since it was a late morning on a Sunday, it didn't seem too appropriate to be fully dressed to the nines. And of course there was the justification for not wanting to take the extra time to put on more makeup. I put some lotion on my hands, took one final glance in the mirror, and headed out the door. It was a perfectly sunny day with only a couple clouds in the sky, and the traffic was fairly quiet, even as I approached the International District. The parking garage was nearly empty and I had my choice of multiple van accessible spots.

Prior to going inside, I sent my friend a quick text letting her know where I was and that I was going to meet Zach. I may be new to this process, but I am fully aware of the safety precautions you need to have when you're meeting someone for the first time. Including strangers you meet online; you have to have that safety net just in case. I took the elevator up to the restaurant and had just enough time to scan the entrance before seeing him down the hallway walking towards me. He was a bit lankier than I anticipated, though to be fair, everyone seems tall to me. He gave a gentle nod and smile as he approached.

"Hi, nice to see you. Thank you for meeting me," he said softly.

"Yeah, thank you too. Shall we go in?" I asked.

"Sure, but I have to tell you. I forgot my wallet, and only realized when I parked. I have a $1.50, so I guess I'll just order some tea."

Seriously? I thought to myself. *Who shows up without their wallet?* I wanted to be polite though, and I had already taken so much effort to prepare for this date, I didn't want to cancel or leave.

So, I smiled again, and said, "Oh, that's okay. We can just get a couple small things," all the while thinking how ridiculous it would be to sit in the middle of dim sum and only order tea.

Dim sum, as it turns out, has many awkward aspects for a first date as well. In summary, these are the lessons I took away from my very first online dating experience:

1) With barely enough time to ask how he was doing, cover the small talk, and get to know each other a bit better, we were interrupted. It's dim sum, so naturally the servers come around with carts of amazing food and ask what you want. There is a deliberation process, decisions to make, and choices to weigh.

2) While dim sum can work if you're vegetarian, it is very difficult if you're a vegan who doesn't consume flour or sugar. I knew he was vegetarian ahead of time and trying to be vegan, but I figured there were enough items available for both of us to eat comfortably, especially if you factored in getting a sesame ball or any number of desserts filled with sweet bean curd. However, that doesn't work if you cut out sugar, flour, and caffeine, so even the tea was out too. I ordered us Chinese broccoli, an entrée off the menu of mixed vegetables with tofu, and one plate of shumai for me. I couldn't go to dim sum without getting at least one item I loved.

3) As more than a beginner, but nowhere near expert, user of chopsticks, Chinese broccoli is nearly impossible to eat. We both eventually caved and used forks, so to avoid any *Pretty Woman* moments with flying broccoli.

Aside from the forgotten wallet and food challenges, the conversation was enjoyable. There were a few awkward silences, but for the most part, we had plenty to discuss. We covered vast territory including family, business endeavors, grad schools, and the pain in the ass that is the GRE. While we discussed a multitude of subjects, we never really ventured past more than the surface of things. We stayed properly on top of the conversation with niceties and pleasantries.

At one point, I asked how he was doing for time.

"I'm teaching a music lesson in an hour and a half."

I grabbed the tea kettle, "Okay, I'll pour another cup of tea."

"Great, I get to enjoy looking at you for a while longer." I smiled and blushed slightly at his sweet comment. I enjoyed the unexpected attention, as small and gentle as it was.

We had a simple goodbye. No hug or kiss, just a smile and, "Thank you so much for meeting me," from him. It was nice and polite with a hint of potential unmentioned romance.

As I waited for the elevator, I found myself thinking that I didn't know where this would go from here, if anywhere. He was nice and I was willing to look past the whole wallet issue, especially since he repeatedly offered to send me money through his online merchant account while I was signing the bill. While we had quite a bit in common, there were several differences, particularly around nutrition and food. Regardless, I felt like this date was an important milestone for me. I found someone online, we met in person at a safe, comfortable place, and it wasn't a total disaster.

Meeting a perfect stranger and sharing a meal with them can be a lovely experience. Sharing your opinions, your thoughts, and your dreams can heighten that experience. When I stop and think about how Zach and I ended up sitting across from each other, I am amazed at all the possibilities that online dating creates.

It can be so difficult to meet new people. Before it might have only been in bars, at work, or through friends and family, and really, what are the odds of meeting anyone of serious potential at a bar? Instead, whenever I would plan to attend a training or join the board of a nonprofit, I would think to myself of the added benefit of meeting new people. Perhaps, I just might meet someone who was single and interesting. After all, a good friend of mine met her fiancé when she attended her first board retreat. It was a true nonprofit fairytale.

My reality, however, was different. I hadn't met anyone new in months. My theories of "putting myself out there" were utterly ineffective. So, while I may not be completely comfortable with this whole online dating thing yet, I am intrigued, curious, and inspired to continue. I want to see where this journey takes me, to experience so many new firsts even as I've become accustomed to a routine of independence and avoidance of settling down.

Sophomore Setback

I can still remember where I was: front passenger seat. My girlfriend was sitting in the back, her boyfriend was driving. We were heading west down 21st, a street I had traveled countless times growing up in Tacoma. It was a cool fall day and we were just getting into the routine of another school year. The sun was warm, but the air was cool and beginning to smell like decaying leaves and pine needles. We were stopped at the light on Proctor. Or maybe it was Stevens. Sometimes, on a cloudy day, they can look the same and over the years this exact detail has itself become a little cloudy. The conversation has stayed with me for more than a decade, even though I may have lost a little of it in translation over the years. It is a story that plays in my head once in awhile, triggered by moments of self-doubt, or maybe even just catching a whiff of those pine needles warmed by the fall sun.

Dana and I had had a few conversations previously about finding me a boyfriend. We had become close our sophomore year, bonding over biology homework assignments and lab projects. I liked her, she was a good friend to me, and we shared a lot of our secret teenage angst with each other. Mostly I liked that she was creative, smart, and interested in all sorts of music, art, and theater. Being around her made me feel like I could explore new interests and not feel so self-conscious. She was in Drama Club and had a very dynamic cadence of speech, raising and lowering her voice, increasing and decreasing

36

the speed in which she spoke, even when just sharing a simple incident that happened in class.

Her boyfriend was a couple years older than we were and had a nice group of friends. They were separate from our high school clique, so I thought there might be some potential for new relationships. I thought that by being separate and older somehow might have afforded them some expanded maturity, tolerance, or empathy. I had romanticized that their age allowed them a more worldly view on life and that they would see me for the truly intelligent and unique being that I was.

The topic of finding me a boyfriend came up in the car. Girlfriends always want their girlfriends to have boyfriends so they can double date. Which only means that then they can see their girlfriend and their boyfriend at the same time, without having to sacrifice one for the other. I am unconvinced it is not for any other reason, my happiness and well-being notwithstanding. Dana, as fun as she was, was no different than anyone else our age that wanted what she wanted without having to give anyone up. If she could spend an afternoon with me and her boyfriend at the same time, she didn't have to make the other feel bad by not being available. If she could find me a boyfriend, especially one of her boyfriend's friends, then the guys would have someone to talk to as well. It was the perfect solution to an age-old dilemma.

We were driving down the road, headed to our favorite park. We were going to feed the ducks and then head to a diner for a little late afternoon fried food indulgence. We had been singing along with a song on the radio until her boyfriend rolled his eyes at us and changed the channel. Amid our fading giggles, Dana pointed out that it might be difficult to find me a match.

"Why?" I asked, quietly. I had been taken aback by her frank comment and I wasn't sure which part of me she thought was such a deterrent. I stared out the window and watched the buildings slide by. I was stunned and uncertain of my ability to control my emotional reaction to her comment. I kept my eyes focused on an invisible point in the distance, one that didn't require me to make eye contact with anyone in the car. I braced myself for her reply, uncertain I was ready to hear it.

"Because dating you will take extra effort. You have to be lifted in and out of the car. Then we have to fold your chair, haul it around to the back and store it in the trunk. That's a lot of work, just to go somewhere." Again, her frankness silenced me.

I was fully aware that there were some activities I simply couldn't do: go for a run, ride a bike, sit in any seat I wanted to in the theater. And yes, it took me longer to do some tasks than people with working legs. But I never considered that to be a burden or a turn off to a potential boyfriend. It's just part of my routine, it's the rhythm of my life. There is a methodical pace to my day, but isn't that true of everyone? Everyone has a route they follow. Some people forge a new path each day, never traversing the same territory twice. And then there are the rest of us that go through the same paces each day. But I guess the shortsightedness of her teenage mind said it like she saw it. Dana saw me and my chair as a burden.

That day, I paid more attention than ever before to how long it took to put my chair together and transfer me from the front seat of the car to my chair when we arrived at the park. And then how hard it was to get the chair over the broken sidewalk around the lake. And then to get me over the grass to the water's edge so we could feed the ducks. All our hustle and bustle had scared the ducks away. It took a patient 15 minutes and a dozen slices of stale bread to convince them to come back and eat what we were giving them.

What's funny, is that in the moment I didn't take the conversation too seriously. I didn't get outwardly upset. I remember being a little quiet. I don't know if or what I said in return or how our conversation ended. Looking back, I know Dana didn't mean to offend or hurt me. If anything, she was being realistic. She was always very practical. At least this is what I have told myself all these years later. Clearly, this notion has stuck with me. A splinter of doubt, shame, and rejection buried so deep within that for many years I had forgotten it was there. It spurred me to adopt certain behaviors that were a response to a notion hidden in my subconscious. The conscious me was being accommodating and making sure not to be an undue burden on my friends. The subconscious me was protecting myself from being hurt again.

It is amazing the mannerisms we learn in order to survive in the social dynamics we create together; cause and effect. Before that moment in the car with Dana I had never really given much thought to the extra work it took to complete daily tasks. From early elementary school, my friends and I seemingly did whatever we wanted, when we wanted. If we wanted to play on the big toy or in the giant, oversized tires, we did – my friends would carry me wherever they were going. Staircases or sidewalk curbs were surmountable. I never thought in terms of limits or boundaries of being in the chair. We were kids being kids. Until we were teenagers and the rules changed.

I don't think my closest friends saw limits either. Yes, it was different that all of my friends could lift me, take me up and down stairs in my chair, and that many of our conversations were not face to face. We got used to talking over my shoulder as they pushed my chair. This was just the way it was. We were all used to it. It was life. It was me. It was what you got when you joined my pack.

Dana and I hadn't met until our freshman year of high school; she hadn't known me since 2nd grade, like my best friend up until that point, Elizabeth. Dana was new to how I maneuvered through life. She didn't seem to mind, but her perspective uncovered the truth about how a potential boyfriend might feel or what they would think about being in a relationship with me. What became apparent was that I had taken for granted and just assumed that my relationships with new people would always resemble those of my childhood. Friends that knew how we moved through life together; new people, friends, or boyfriends wouldn't have that same perspective. They would have to learn how to be with me. This was new information for my analytical mind to process. They wouldn't have the years of practice, comfort, and acceptance. Could it ever be just a normal way of life for them or would it always be burdensome?

After that moment in the car with Dana, I spent many years being hyper-aware of making people wait for me, or taking up too much of their time. I spent countless hours planning out my days, making sure I wasn't a burden to anyone, that I could do for myself what I needed, and in record time. I've always strived to be as independent as possible. But I do have limits. Undeniably. There is no changing certain facts. With these thoughts, that tiny splinter of a memory can re-emerge just enough to send a sudden, sharp, pierce of pain. Always brief, but always there.

My Place on the Pedestal

My Best Friend's Wedding is a romantic comedy with Julia Roberts and Cameron Diaz. Julia plays the role of best friend (Julianne) to Michael, a guy whom she once unsuccessfully dated but ended up staying best friends with for many years. Michael announces that he's getting married to Kim (Cameron Diaz) and begs Julianne to hold his hand through the process. Meanwhile, Kim asks Julianne to be her maid of honor all while Julianne realizes she has true romantic feelings for Michael. A scene that has always stuck with me is where Julianne and Kim are alone in an elevator for the first time after meeting each other. Kim hits the emergency stop button and essentially confronts Julianne about her overprotective nature, her reasons for being there, and then ultimately says, *"You win."*

Julianne is shocked and says, *"I didn't see that coming."*

"He's got you on a pedestal and me in his arms," Kim retorts.

Why did this scene resonate with me so much? Too often, I found myself in relationships with guys, in which they would have me on the proverbial pedestal – the one who was perfect, brilliant, caring, and would always be there for him, but would never be the one for him. I was on the pedestal, I had won, but he'd be marrying the girl in his arms. I was the best friend. I knew their insecurities, the challenges they faced with their parents, the deep struggles they had.

They would talk with me for hours. I could tell from the inflection in their voice when they were on the verge of losing their temper or breaking down completely. They wholeheartedly trusted me. I was the one they spoke to about the girl they were interested in or in love with or had just broken up with and about whom they were still devastated.

Being placed on the pedestal was not a one-time occurrence with one boy. The pattern happened with many while growing up, but one in particular was the hardest…the most frustrating…the most crushing at times.

As early as sixth grade I remember him telling me how great I was. Brad would call me daily. We attended the same after school program and would hangout every day. We liked the same music and we could talk for hours on the phone. He would sing to me on the phone and complain about his dad. I thought he was the smartest person I had ever met. He was very protective of me too; he would always give me the third degree if I mentioned some other guy talking to me at school. He told me I was beautiful and brilliant. Yet, he would also tell me about the girl he thought was gorgeous and amazing. I waited patiently during the periods when he wouldn't call because he was with her, and then listen even more patiently after the break up as he talked about all that had gone wrong.

I had once confessed my feelings for him, and he told me he saw me as a best friend. It was in these moments, as they repeated in my life, that I was reminded of the song "Save the Best for Last" by Vanessa Williams.

In the song, Vanessa recounts how the guy would always come to her after breakups and she'd wonder how he could share his dreams with her but not love her. Eventually, the guy sees the light just when she's about to give up on him; he goes and saves the best for last. However, Brad never saw the light, even though he would at times make comments about how beautiful I was or even how he loved me. Typically, such comments would be said the moment I began to express interest in someone else. Granted, some of this back and forth occurred during the overly dramatic years of middle school and high school, but nonetheless, the minute I began slipping away, he would reel me back in. It was confusing for me. After all, we had so much in common. We connected and understood each other.

I can clearly recall the intense conversations we would have during the long car rides we would take on clear, chilly nights. We'd head out on the quieter highway through the port of Tacoma, and weave our way through Brown's Point to the lighthouse. Our favorite songs would be blasting from the speakers, and I would think to myself, perhaps we're finally on the same page, and he might actually feel the way I'm feeling tonight. We'd sit, looking out at the stars, listening to song after song; it was like Charlie in *The Perks of Being a Wallflower* when he said he felt "infinite" during that perfect moment with his friends with the perfect song playing in the background. In the book, the song that was playing was never shared, but in the film, the song was "Heroes" by David Bowie. For me, it was "Zombie" by the Cranberries or "Runaway Train" by Soul Asylum.

Brad never reciprocated that night or any other night. Often, he'd even disappear after that perfect night under the stars; he'd stop calling me and ignore my calls. No emails either. Just silence. Eventually, he would emerge as if nothing had happened, as if we had been in constant contact. He'd start sharing his plans for after high school and who he was thinking of asking to the prom. I was back to being Julianne. He was still looking for Kim and so it was until the day many years later when he finally did marry the woman of his dreams.

I remember one night when Brad picked me up at the dorm during my freshman year of college. We went for another one of our infamous and final car rides. He was moving out of state with his then girlfriend and eventual future wife. He thanked me for being his best friend. For listening to and supporting him, and then he said something I always knew, but never wanted to believe.

He started, "I know I was never fair to you."

I just listened, while looking straight ahead through the windshield. I knew I couldn't look at him while he spoke or rather, I didn't want him to see me, my eyes.

"I never had full feelings for you, but I never wanted you to be with anyone else. I treated you like you were mine, even though I wouldn't be yours...I was an ass. I'm sorry."

I felt a small lump in my throat. I continued to stare out at the stars above, and I nodded slightly. I couldn't say anything. My face began to feel the heat that occurs when I know I'm close to crying. The stars blurred from the tears that were beginning to form. I forced myself to bring the stars back into focus – to push the few tears back. They *were not* going to escape down my cheeks. I was not going to let Brad see the tears...the hurt...the disappointment, especially since this was all about the past. He had been with his girlfriend for a year now and it just didn't make sense for me to be this upset. Yet, he had finally validated how I had experienced our entire relationship. He also fully confirmed what I had known intuitively all along, but tried so hard to ignore. I was never the one for him.

It is flattering to be on the pedestal. To have others hold you in such high regard. It boosts the self-esteem to hear that others see you as confident, service-oriented, and beautiful. You realize the power you have to make the world a better place, and you understand that others recognize this ability in you and admire or love you for it. But there is only room for one on the pedestal. It is lonely and cold up there. Yes, others might believe you are well-positioned to affect tremendous change from where you sit, but ultimately I wind up looking down at the world around me, at the couples holding each other in their arms.

I start to wonder...doubt...*would I, could I, ever be the one in someone else's arms?*

Fumbling Through Alone

Having worked with youth for many years, I have learned and seen the power that musicians, actors, actresses, and mainstream media have on the impressionable minds of young people. I was equally influenced by such media growing up whether by subliminally understanding what it meant to be considered beautiful in today's society or overtly wanting to emulate certain favorite characters. Regardless of the positive and negative impacts of media, as youth we look to others, our friends, our idols, our mentors and teachers, and yes, even fictional characters or the real people behind them, for guidance, affirmation, or inspiration. We look to them to help us understand and make sense of our own experiences. However, one model was noticeably absent for me and it wasn't until I finally gave in to watching the TV series *Glee* that I realized what I had been missing. We'll come back to *Glee* in a minute.

I can recall only a few instances of seeing characters on TV who used wheelchairs other than the occasional scenes of patients being pushed around in chairs during hospital visits. When I was very young, I remember seeing parts of the movie *Heidi* in which the grandfather deliberately leaves the girl (Clara) in the wheelchair alone in the mountains. In my head, the scene was much more dramatic with the man throwing the girl out of the wheelchair and she miraculously begins to walk, simply because she always could. I was terrified at the thought of someone believing this method would work. I hadn't known anyone that I thought would try, although Madeline used to jokingly refer to this scene as she carried me up stairs, all while asking if I just hadn't tried hard enough to walk.

Then there was a character in a short-lived TV series called *Dark Angel* featuring Jessica Alba and Michael Weatherly. I don't remember much of the series, but Logan was the name of the character who used a wheelchair and there was an obvious romantic connection between him and Jessica Alba's character (Max). I was fascinated to see their relationship unfold, but remember being disappointed when eventually Logan was able to walk and I believe it was only after his recovery that he finally kissed Max and started a relationship with her.

The third and final example I can recall from childhood was *Notting Hill* with Hugh Grant and Julia Roberts. Two of Hugh Grant's friends were a married couple and the wife (Bella) used a wheelchair. In one scene, the couple is saying goodnight to some house guests, and they show Max, Bella's husband, pick her up and carry her up the stairs. I was intrigued to see a married couple of an able bodied man and a woman in a wheelchair. I was equally curious of a husband so willing to help his wife. But I didn't understand why he picked her up out of the wheelchair to take her upstairs instead of just pulling her up the stairs in her chair. Was there another chair up there? Would he eventually bring her chair upstairs (the film never showed him doing that)? If not, was she just stuck wherever he set her down? The implied details didn't make sense to me, and clearly the film directors hadn't thought through such logistics.

The poignant moment for me though was when Hugh Grant's character was rushing to catch the woman of his dreams before she left the country. All his friends were trying to help, and they piled into one car to start the chase. In the scene, Max is in the front passenger seat when he asks where Bella is. They say she's not coming, and he immediately tells them to hold on. He jumps out of the car, goes around the other side and picks her up. As she says, *"No, it's okay,"* he just smiles, says *"Come on, babe,"* and sets her in the car. They fold her wheelchair, throw it in the back of the car, and drive off. That will always be my favorite scene of the whole movie.

These are the best examples I can recall seeing anyone who remotely reflected the nature of my existence in mainstream media while I was growing up. Not much to go on when you're a teenager thinking about relationships or kissing or just trying to make it through high school without any relevant or applicable role models. While television rarely depicts life accurately, having such examples are important elements of our culture and there was a noticeable absence of anyone who looked like me in skin tone, ethnicity, or ability in the media. Then came *Glee* and the character known as Arty, who uses a wheelchair.

I first watched *Glee* at age 29, and the emotions it brought to the surface at times surprised me. They were experiences I had much forgotten about. In one episode, the school decides not to pay for a bus with a wheelchair lift to transport the Glee Club to a competition. The other members say it's okay because Arty's dad could just drive him separately. Arty finally admits that this form of exclusion hurt his feelings. These are key experiences you miss when you can't participate like everyone else and they stick with you.

During my junior year of high school, I participated in a nationally based program to travel and experience Washington D.C. I was so excited to go and several friends from my class were going as well. This was my first cross-country trip with friends and I was ecstatic. The excitement was immediately diminished from the moment I arrived at the airport. I had travelled many times, but it hadn't occurred to me that I would be separated from my friends during the boarding process. I am almost always boarded first since I require the use of an aisle chair. However, to make matters worse, the flight crew and skycaps insisted on changing my seat to one behind the bulkhead, while *all* my classmates and even the teacher were seated together in the back. I made the best of it, found the positive, and got some sleep on the red-eye flight. This was something the rest of the class didn't get since they were all giggly, chattering, and making memories together in their group section. So while I may have gotten some sleep, I still missed out on the camaraderie of being among my classmates.

The flight was just the first of a ridiculous amount of rules and guidelines I'd have to endure that the program had in place for hosting students with disabilities. The end result was that I absolutely hated the trip and multiple times each day had to fight back tears of frustration and anger. From always having to go through separate or back entrances to taking the special van or bus instead of the charter bus that carried my friends, I frequently found myself alone or in the company of the program assistant assigned to help me manage my accessibility needs. I cannot recall the details of visiting the monuments or the conference we attended at the State Department. Even seeing the White House was a blur. Instead, what I remember is being stuck with the program assistant and his insistence on taking me backwards through doorways and elevators even though I kept offering, begging even to go forwards and that I could push myself to do so. But, no, it was policy and he didn't "take orders" from students. I had never felt more excluded, less than, different, and helpless.

Back to *Glee*. It was the first time I had ever seen someone bend over to give a person in a wheelchair a first kiss. Growing up, I used to wonder how a first kiss would go. I could try to imagine it, but I never saw it. Of the countless kisses on TV, not one ever reflected what a first kiss would be like *for me*.

In another scene, Arty's girlfriend picks him up and lays him on the bed, and I thought to myself, *Wow!* Someone who has never been introduced to a person with a disability can see how sex could work with them. Here is an example. Of course, the specific details were glossed over, but the acknowledgement that people with disabilities have sex drives, can have sex, and can enjoy sex were what excited me the most. It was a new model to think about. Perhaps future generations of teenage girls and boys with physical disabilities will no longer have to have such awkward conversations with able-bodied counterparts about whether they can have sex or not. Of course, everyone's situation and abilities are different, but it has amazed me how often I have had to correct people's assumptions about sex. A little help from the media, regardless of inaccuracies and innuendos, is a welcome relief.

I think it has been said that in many ways *Will & Grace* allowed for more open discussion and awareness of homosexuality, aside from any criticisms of the show. It was a new model to consider. Were there exaggerations here and there? Sure, but the show helped set a new positive tone and paved the way for greater acceptance on a broader scale. The power of media has its occasional upsides. In similar fashion, for me it seems that *Glee* has been the closest to exposing the types of experiences people with disabilities, both physically and developmentally, have. Directly and indirectly, *Glee* is helping to change perceptions of what it means to be a teenage girl with down's syndrome or a boy using a wheelchair and trying to fit in.

The Torture of the Unknown

I have always enjoyed the TV series *Friends* and those closest to me know that I will on occasion refer to one of the characters or a scene as if they were part of real life. I usually do this for reference or comparison, and mostly for a little chuckle. A trend has emerged since starting the whole online dating thing. I liken my experience to a particular episode that tells my story quite well. I'll let the *Friends* cast set the stage for me.

In one episode, Rachel's boss meets Chandler and she asks Rachel to set them up. Chandler agrees to go on a date, but then decides to not call her, even though he said he would, because he really isn't interested in her. The next day, Rachel's boss raves about how well the date went and that she can't wait to hear from him. Of course, Chandler never calls and thus starts the obsession. Rachel, caught in the middle, finds Chandler after work and begs him to call, mimicking her boss: *Why, hasn't he called, Rachel? He said he would call. Why hasn't he called? Why, Rachel, why?*

In my online dating experiences so far, the responses and follow through have been all over the map. I have always had an analytical mind and in some ways this is a good trait to have. I'm able to look at situations from multiple perspectives, to hypothesize possible explanations for certain occurrences and to empathize with others. However, this skill is absolutely my worst enemy when it comes to dating. With an analytical mind also comes a logical mind, which doesn't always equate to a healthy combination. I *know* logically that trying to understand people's behavior, such as why they have chosen to respond or not, is pointless. Yet, turning off the proverbial analytical switch is incredibly challenging, particularly when there are a whole bunch of emotions – excitement, anxiety, anticipation – swirling about and preventing any sort of clarity in my otherwise clear head.

The questions, the hypothesizing, and the pondering are ceaseless.

Why hasn't he written back? Was it something I wrote? Did I divulge too much? Maybe I shouldn't have shared that I still have a VHS player.

The waiting game is relentless and tormenting. As the time clicks by, I start trying to identify patterns in the emails sent thus far. *Hmm, 4 out of the 6 emails were sent around 4pm. Okay, it's 3:30 right now, so perhaps I'll hear from him in half an hour.* 4:30 comes and goes.

My mind continues to hypothesize. *Well, that one time, he emailed at 9:30. What day was that? Tuesday. Oh, so he must just work late on Tuesdays.*

Perhaps he met someone else already. Or maybe he had a chance encounter with Big Foot and didn't make it out alive?

This very well could have been the case for one guy I was writing to who just disappeared completely. He said he was really into Big Foot and spent much of his time hiking in the mountains – not necessarily in search of said creature, but with the hope that he might happen across one. We had a nice exchange of emails, and then *poof!* Silence.

Then of course, I wonder what the rules are around communicating after a 1st date. If you don't hear from someone within 24 hours, is that a bad sign? What about 48 hours?

There's a scene from the movie *You've Got Mail* with Meg Ryan and Tom Hanks. The two have been writing each other anonymously and eventually agree to meet. What they don't realize at first, but Tom Hanks discovers later in the movie, is that they in fact know each other in 'real life' and are sworn enemies. He stands her up because of his realization, knowing they could never get along outside of the virtual world. The next day, Meg's character recounts the tale to her friends who then start hypothesizing why he didn't show up. They finally conclude that he was the serial killer who'd been outsmarting police for weeks until that very night she was supposed to meet her mystery man. Ergo, he didn't show up because he had been arrested.

These scenarios, where a guy seems interested, but hasn't even hinted at getting together and meeting in person happens in the online dating world quite often. At least enough for me to notice. My working theories go in the following order:

1) He's a serial killer (thank you Meg Ryan)

2) He's married (or has one or more girlfriends)

3) He still lives with his parents and is waiting for them to go out of town

4) Some combination of 1, 2, and 3

These are the theories I come up with to address the questions I don't have answers to and while I imagine other online daters have hypotheses of their own, I don't think anyone really knows for sure. So what do you do? The only strategy I've come up with is to consciously catch myself when I'm having these thoughts. If I ask myself a question about why I haven't heard from someone, I respond with: *Who knows, but there's no point in dwelling on it.* If that fails, I simply think of the Beatles' song "Let it Be." After all, if there's nothing else you can do, you may as well just sing. You know the song. Try humming it the next time you're anxious or your mind won't stop reeling with questions and theories and more questions. Trust me, the song helps.

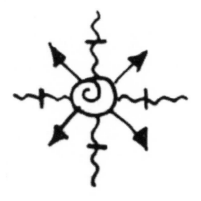

From Fearful to Fantastic:
The One Who Taught Me Sex Could be Amazing

I was always very private about my emotions or interest in guys. I partook in conversations with friends about crushes, but more often than not I would just listen to their stories. If I deeply liked someone, I kept it to myself. Similarly, I could talk about sex, but I didn't share many details about my sex life or lack thereof. If I did, I sometimes exaggerated to save face, made up certain details, or shared only part of the story. The truth was, I was generally behind most of my girlfriends when it came to sex. My first real kiss happened in 8th grade, while several friends had theirs in elementary school. While some of my girlfriends were still virgins in high school, many were not. I felt the pressure to keep up, particularly when starting college. Sex for me started out on the wrong foot. It had not been the magical moment it was supposed to be, that I had been promised it would be. I imagined it differently, as I am sure most women do. And it took quite some time to find that sensual balance.

It was the first week of college. I had it all planned out. Brent was going to come out on Friday. Brent had been my friend with benefits through high school. He had been my "first" for just about all of my sexual experiences to that point. We had started with phone sex. We shared incredible fantasies. They were exhilarating and I knew that sex with him was going to be wonderful. For sure, I understood how first times are generally awkward or painful even, but eventually you get to the realm of amazing, right? Sure, it's rare for two people to click immediately, but I was still convinced that our chemistry and attraction for each other would overcome such obstacles. After all, he had discovered a secret weakness – a point of pleasure that when kissed sent me reeling. How could he not be good with everything else?

His intricate descriptions during our phone conversations of what he'd do if we were together were just that: descriptions, words, one dimensional promises. When we were finally together, it all boiled down to "I want you so bad" with a few quick kisses, a rapid and clumsy tearing off of my shirt, and lightening-pace removal of my bra. There wasn't any foreplay. There wasn't any anticipation. There wasn't any time to warm up to each other. Add to the ambience my extreme nervousness, a lack of lubricant, and it was brutally clear – this was going to end in disaster.

The pain was beyond anything I had imagined. I gently told him to stop, which he quickly obliged. We lay looking at each other, dumbfounded, embarrassed, and deflated. There were no supportive words. He suggested trying a different position. We tried, without much improvement. Eventually, I told him I was tired and needed to stop. We took a break. It was the middle of the afternoon when he had come crashing through my door and he was staying the night. This was proving to be a long arduous day. We got dressed and went to dinner. All the while, I felt embarrassed and ashamed that it hadn't gone well. We tried again that night with similar results. I couldn't believe how painful and unsuccessful we were at trying to enjoy our time together. We eventually resorted to 3rd base to make sure he got some satisfaction. That night it never dawned on me that he should have returned the favor.

The second time wasn't any better. Perhaps it was the insensitive friend with benefits who I thought was more sincere than he really was. I was young and naïve at the time and see now how I misread a few situations. Regardless of said partners, the deep rooted fear was that something was inherently wrong with me. I secretly wondered if the polio caused me to be deficient somehow, that I would never be able to enjoy sex. Since I was such a private person, I never spoke about this with anyone either. I remember reading one short paragraph in a human sexuality textbook that glossed over the topic with a slight mention of how people with polio could have sex, but certain positions may be difficult. If I remember correctly, I think the authors recommended the missionary position. That was the sole bit of information I had on the matter at the time. I never felt comfortable talking with doctors. I could not fathom the idea of talking about it with my mom. Not that I couldn't, I didn't want to. When I mentioned it to friends I would get advice and suggestions, but never more information about my situation specifically. I could have researched it online, but I was so inwardly focused at the time, and worried that there was something wrong with me, that perhaps subconsciously I didn't do any research because I was afraid of what the answer might be. The nagging fear was that maybe I wouldn't be able to enjoy sex. Ever.

I had tried having sex with two partners, and with each one we just couldn't seem to make things work. So, I started avoiding sex. My rationalizing mind started to take over. I began to think that I just didn't like sex. I kept relationships in a third base holding pattern, and since most of my partners up until this point had only been casual relationships, often times we were never together long enough to get to a point where it was expected that we start sleeping together, so I was off the hook and continued to act as if sex didn't matter to me. Besides, I was always afraid of getting pregnant, so by not having sex, I didn't have to worry about it. I didn't have to worry about birth control. I discovered the joys of just making out. I loved foreplay. I didn't mind giving oral sex and that seemed to be sufficient for the guys I was with.

Then came the one. The one who was patient and knew how to make me feel comfortable, safe. It really did matter *who* I was with even though I wanted to believe otherwise. The clichés about finding the right person to be intimate with were in fact true. Yet, it wasn't just about having an emotional connection. I soon learned that what mattered more was a level of respect, care, and concern that each holds for the other. He was reassuring and instructive. He knew that having extra lubricant would be useful.

"Relax. Breathe. Again. Breathe in. Exhale. Breathe in," he repeated.

I remember saying something to the effect that sex with me required some additional effort.

His reply was simply, "You are worth it."

Our first time was not great, but for a few minutes, it wasn't bad either. Our second time was better. By the third time, I felt absolutely free. Sex was fun, and I could enjoy it. I loved it! How had I not been experiencing sex like this all along? It was a huge relief. It seemed to me a very long road to travel, a lot of exploration and learning the hard way, but I was able to conclude that there wasn't something broken about me after all.

The CM Ratio

Despite my insecurities, there are some aspects of my body in which I have come to take great pride. My smile is one. My breasts are another. As senior year of high school wrapped up and college began, I discovered the wonder of the low-cut top that showed off my cleavage. This amazing invention allowed me to pretend that the only features people would look at were my breasts and my smile, if I framed them both. Perhaps then they would be blind to other physical characteristics that I felt were flawed. If I distracted them visually, then maybe they would like me before passing judgment and dismissing me because of all the things that were wrong with me, like my funny thighs.

I started with strappy, rounded neck tank tops accompanied by black skirts. The black backdrop camouflaged by legs and waist and made me feel like they were hidden, covered, devoid of detail and hopefully overlooked. I eventually graduated to plunging V-neck blouses and became the master of leveraging my bountiful assets. I had figured out how to draw attention away from the less flattering parts of my body to the general "triangle of awesomeness" created by my smile and breasts. I was proud of my cleavage, even if that was all they saw, and my smile was always ready to catch their attention if they happened to look up or decide to move away from my chest. It was a good system.

In college, it was common for my guy friends and dorm-mates to give hugs, massages, and other forms of physical attention and affection. For me, they were mostly platonic, but I discovered an interesting positive correlation. The more cleavage I showed, the longer the massage I received. What this meant was that for a moment someone was touching me, appreciating my body in a harmless way. A male was paying attention to me and I knew how to control it, how to manipulate it, and how to reap the benefits of drawing some positive attention to myself. Thus, the CM (Cleavage:Massage) ratio was born and taken full advantage of during my undergrad years.

Here's how the CM ratio worked:
Zero cleavage might equal just a quick squeeze of the shoulders or a quick little massage while being asked how my day was going.

Business cleavage afforded a longer period of time, say five or ten minutes, of muscular hands working the knots out of my shoulders and neck. For a girl using a chair, this was important physical therapy combined with the attention I enjoyed from a guy. Pushing a chair every day requires constant engagement of many muscles. You know, the Trapezius, Omohyoid, and Sternocleidomastoid. They work so hard all day long that a ten-minute massage provides a great deal of relief.

Girls Night Out cleavage guaranteed to bring at least 20-minutes of intense massage. The kind of massage that includes fingers stretching ever so carefully so as to work the upper pectoralis major on either side of my neck and chest. Because as many men know, all muscles are connected, and the wider surface area you cover, the further you go from the source, the better the quality of the massage. Not to mention, the view from their perspective is all cleavage and lingerie, which can be distracting and cause them to lose all sense of time.

After college I realized that this tactic wasn't always appropriate, even though I felt like I had mastered the technique and found entertainment and satisfaction in using it. If I wasn't dating, if I wasn't 100% comfortable in my own skin, at least I was getting some attention. If no one was falling in love with me, or asking me out on dates, at least they were aware of my femininity. When I entered the professional world I had to do some adjusting of the CM ratio system. It wasn't appropriate to show the girls in the same way as before.

Enter the utility of adjustable cleavage tops. This usually included a zip sweater or button-up shirt that I could wear over the low-cut camisoles. When working, attending staff meetings, or training, I had a fully covered chest. If I had a work event where youth or families weren't present, I would employ the business cleavage: I would open the sweater or buttoned shirt to reveal just enough for anyone with decent observation skills to notice my assets. My appropriate-meter was to determine if it would be uncomfortable if my dad were around. A father's eyes are always so discerning and a good barometer for appropriate behavior.

The next level of exposure was savored for nights out with the girls when I employed the extreme tactic of wearing tops that had color-coordinated bras beneath them. There was no way anyone was going to miss seeing at least a portion of the center of the bra in the dip of the v-neck. My favorite was a sky blue short-sleeved top with a beautiful burgundy demi-cup from Victoria's Secret. I felt sexy, sophisticated, and my confidence soared in this outfit. I felt good, I knew I looked good, and I always got the attention that I wanted when I wore it out.

While I knew I was primarily creating opportunities for surface level attraction – that I was letting people be drawn to me for physical characteristics rather than for who I really was – a smart, thoughtful, caring, empathetic woman – I found it important to have these moments of feeling truly sexy. So often, glimpses of myself in the mirror resulted in affirmation of all the things that I thought were wrong with my body: a bit chubby, wide flat funny thighs, awkwardly skinny ankles, a short torso, and the list goes on. The times when I'd push the CM ratio to its fullest potential I was able to forget all my shortcomings. I was able to appreciate my body for its strengths, albeit only a few strengths in my mind at the time. I knew it wasn't a permanent thing. The next morning, I'd still be the "full me" but those temporary boosts of confidence brought on by leveraging the

CM ratio provided much needed reprieves from the deluge of negative thoughts and self-talk. These were my pep talks to myself and a way to momentarily mute the voices of my relentless inner critic. I employed a system that I knew worked to lift my self-esteem and allowed me to truly enjoy an evening without a care in the world, a second thought, or a question of my ability to fit in the world. These nights formed some of my favorite memories with good friends, enjoying life exactly as it was; feeling sexy and beautiful at the same time.

What a Lovely Punching Bag!

It was my junior year at college, and I had been hired as a German tutor through Academic Assistance. During the second week of the school year, I was sitting in the library during my office hours. No one had signed up for that day, so I was prepping for the upcoming German conversation hour when he arrived. Blonde, blue eyes, not too tall, and slim.

He gave a shy smile as he introduced himself, "Hi, I'm Mitchell, are you the German tutor?"

"Yes, yes I am. I'm Sheely. Nice to meet you Mitchell," I felt myself unable to stop smiling. "How can I help you?"

"I'm in Professor Hollin's German 101 class. I'm already feeling a bit lost."

"Ah yes, she can be tough, but you'll learn so much in her class, and I'm here to help."

"Great, can I sign up for regular sessions?"

"Yes, but you can only have one officially scheduled session each week. You can always stop by during office hours though and if no one else has signed up, you can take an open slot."

"Okay. Thank you. Where do I sign up?"

I passed him the sign-up form, and watched as he signed up for every Monday at 1:30. I was giddy inside. This tutoring job was going to be fantastic. We weren't really supposed to date anyone we tutored, but that didn't mean I couldn't enjoy the view, right? Besides, I wasn't too worried because he was a sophomore and I wasn't really looking to date someone younger than me.

Mitchell was very formal and polite for the first several tutoring sessions, but he was ever so curious about my life. Each session, he'd ask me increasingly personal questions. Starting initially with my academic track, then venturing into where I grew up, why I chose my major and my minor, what I wanted to do after graduating. He was planning to study abroad in Germany the following year.

As the semester progressed, our conversations became more fluid and natural. He frequently stopped by Wednesdays or Fridays during my office hours. At least half the time he'd find me with an open session. He was perceptive, observant. He once commented that I always wear my hair pulled back when it rains, then asked me why. His accuracy caught me off guard. I smiled and gave a slight laugh as I shared that my hair gets super frizzy and curly when it gets wet, so I keep it in a ponytail on rainy days. He nodded in understanding, but then said he guessed my hair was probably still exquisite even if I was caught in a storm with my hair down. Any time he made such observations or compliments, I would feel myself blush, smile, and shake my head, as if trying to shake off the feeling of being exposed, a bit vulnerable, and complimented all at the same time.

One Monday afternoon, I had just come from my cognitive psych class after receiving some not so positive feedback on my final project. It was still early enough in the semester to make changes, but it had been a painful conversation.

I was looking over the notes from the last tutoring session when he arrived.

"Hey, how's it going?" I asked as I smiled like I always did when he arrived.

"I'm good, but what's wrong? What happened?"

I was jolted for a second and a bit confused.

"Hmm?" I looked at him inquisitively.

He repeated, "What's wrong? Something happened."

I shook my head, "No, nothing's wrong. I'm okay. C'mon, let's get started. The mid-term is coming up faster than you think."

He insisted, "No, you're upset. I can see it in your eyes. You can tell me."

He looked at me, as I stared back, thinking, how could he possibly know? I hadn't been crying. I was frustrated and upset, sure, but it wasn't that bad. I could tell he wasn't going to let it go.

"I just had a rough class. It's okay, really."

"Alright, I'll let it go for now."

We proceeded with reviewing vocabulary and adjective endings. There were moments, as I was looking at and pointing to sections in the book that I'd catch him just looking at me with concern...with care. I ignored his glances.

I was only tutoring for an hour that day, and his session was the last one. Mitchell offered to walk me back to my dorm. I was hesitant, but it was also raining, and having someone push would definitely be faster. I reluctantly agreed, knowing that he would return to the subject of why I was upset. It wasn't that I cared so much about him knowing what I was upset about. Rather, it was the fact that he knew I was upset in the first place that got me; he seemed to genuinely care.

Against my better judgment, I confirmed that I was in fact upset and shared the details as we ducked the rain drops under the cover of the colorful fall leaves. He ever so gently squeezed my shoulder at one point, and I felt a shiver through my body. I knew I was in trouble. I was beginning to like him too much.

Anytime he had the last session on my schedule he would walk me back to my dorm or to my next class. We started talking more freely; sharing more personal details. He could always put a smile on my face, and our walks usually ended with him telling me a story of some random misadventure he had had with his brother or group of friends. He had grown up in Kirkland, and was now living with his older brother in Renton.

I soon found myself just waiting for our next tutoring session, and we had starting emailing between sessions. Initially, they were school-focused, but it wasn't long before we were sharing about our favorite music or places to eat or anything else that was on our minds. We would have "flash forwards" in which we'd talk about having a house in Germany or Austria when we were older – it was a debate between Cologne or Vienna. I loved both cities.

Eventually, the flash forwards included details about where we'd live in the States, how many children we'd have and where they would go to school. We talked a lot about us both being graduated and being able to live and be together. In our email exchanges, we had agreed that it would not be a good idea for us to officially date, at least not publicly. I know this contributed to the thrill and intrigue of our interactions, especially since technically any relationship was forbidden while I was his tutor. To add to the complications, his family was adamant about him staying focused on school. He had some challenging relationships in his past, one of which almost caused him to drop out of high school; college was much more costly and they weren't going to have any of that. The only way he was able to move out of his parent's house while attending college was by his brother's promise to keep him in check.

Although Mitch was just a year behind me, he was two years younger in age. However, he could still astound me with his maturity and intuition. He could read me like a book, understanding page by page the details of my life. Yet, we had some key differences, including religion. He had chosen our school because of its faith based foundation, whereas I chose to attend despite that fact. While our age difference was minimal, it also meant that I could legally drink while he could not – this would prove challenging as my friends and I frequented the late night Power Hour at The Ram, a local restaurant and bar, every Monday night in addition to a host of other 21 and older locales on the weekends.

Yet, we made it work. I couldn't believe the thoughts I was having about marriage and children and the real discussions we would have about how we'd manage finances or what modifications we'd make to our house to make it accessible, while still being beautifully designed. He taught me (I was a reluctant student at first) that it was okay to share my problems, to ask him for help, to be supported and to dream out loud.

"I need you to realize that we're a team. I can help. We can work this out together," he'd tell me when I was holding back again about some issue at work.

I struggled though because publicly we were still pretending to be just friends and privately we were having an emotional affair of the heart. To make things more complex, we had agreed that we didn't want to hold each other back from our dreams and aspirations. At the time, I was contemplating grad school out of state, and he wanted to study abroad for a full year if he could manage it. We knew we would have some extended periods of time in which we'd be separated, so we tried to keep things simple, but it was clear – I was definitely in love.

We said *I love you* every time we said good night on the phone. He called me *sweetheart* and *my love*. In emails, he'd tell me how smart I was and what song he heard that made him think of me. There were countless songs that were ours, but one of my favorites was "You Belong to Me" performed by Jason Wade of Lifehouse, the *Shrek* version.

He'd send me an encouraging text before an exam: "You're gonna ace it! Love, Me".

Around spring break though, something started to change in our relationship. The sweet encouraging emails and long phone conversations had begun to be replaced with sarcasm and criticisms. The changes were subtle and intermittent at first, but they gradually became the rule, rather than the exception.

"You're such a perfectionist. Would a 'B' kill you?" he'd retort as I commented on being stressed out about an upcoming exam.

"Your mom is visiting you *again*?" he'd ask in an incredulous tone. The theme of me being too dependent on my parents would continue to develop over the coming months.

Then, he'd suddenly revert to be being the sweet, kind, and caring guy he was in the beginning. He was like those commercials for sour candies that say, *"First they're sour, then they're sweet"* as they show an oversized gummy bear shaped candy causing a raucous and then offering an innocent hug. It was not uncommon for him to say something snide or rude as he dropped me off at the dorm. Only for me to get to my room and find a Post-It on my desk with a single green, peanut M&M placed in the center of a hand-drawn heart; he knew they were my favorite. The whole message would read, "I <3 you."

This was my Mitchell. Aggravating and sweet, hurtful and helpful, mean and loving. As time progressed, I found myself never really knowing which Mitchell was going to be on the other end of the phone or which Mitchell was going to walk me to my car as I headed to work. Our tutoring sessions became the only times when he would be peaceful...respectful...and mostly kind with the occasional eye-roll or shake of the head thrown in for good measure.

Looking back, it took me longer than I'd like to admit to realize the type of relationship I was in. I didn't see how I was starting to doubt myself, to feel less than worthy, to blame myself for not making *him* happy. I had always been self-conscious about my inadequacies physically, but now I was starting to feel smaller...weaker...in personality, intelligence, independence; all the qualities and aspects of myself that I had previously never seen as deficient. I found myself becoming resentful and intentionally saying things in return to be hurtful or to act as if I cared less about what he said. I didn't like the person I was becoming when I was around him. Much later, I heard the song "Please Don't Leave Me" by Pink which described our situation well.

For me, I fit the lines about being obnoxious and wondering what it was about him that made me act so mean and nasty, when I'm not normally that way.

For him, it was in the lyrics where he'd tell me how wonderful or beautiful I was while simultaneously making it clear that I was the target of his frustrations. Of course, he'd immediately apologize and say he needed me and that he couldn't be without me.

I never left these interactions with Mitch without feeling like I had been punched, beaten up on the inside. My ego, my heart, my stomach; they all felt bruised after these moments together.

The biggest heartbreak, and finally the beginning of the end for me, was during the middle of my senior year. I was working for an after school program nearby, and I absolutely loved the job. Unfortunately, around November the organization ran into some financial troubles and started making significant budget cuts. The leadership team was under tremendous pressure to do more with less, but I found myself disagreeing with many of the decisions being made. One key staff member was placed on the chopping block, and I found myself wanting to resign in protest, wholeheartedly against the decision. It was more than the fact that he made the program what it was; it was more systemic than that. The organization also chose to reduce scholarships, eliminate the extended after hours, and nearly doubled the monthly program fees overnight. On a business level, I could understand the budget demands that called for such changes, but from a personal perspective, this was no longer the program I had once loved.

Every day was filled with stress and anxiety about who would be next to go and we were increasingly limited in the ways we could support our youth. We could no longer offer bus passes for our latch key kids to get home unless he or she had their parents demonstrate financial need. It wasn't enough that the long walk home without bus fare was dangerous, cold, and dark regardless of parent's financial stability. For those families that could perhaps afford it, but chose not to, their child suffered immeasurably because we couldn't make budget decisions based on the mission and vision of the program. Once the care and well being of the youth in the program were potentially at risk, I finally decided enough was enough. I was going to quit. Even though I had it rationalized and planned out, it was still the most difficult decision I had made in my young adult life. I loved the youth I worked with each day. I hated the idea of no longer being there, no longer being able to see them each day and make sure they were doing their homework, answering their questions, playing games with them, or just spending time talking to them because they mattered. They were the most important part of my afternoons. Sadly, I knew I couldn't stay. I gave my 2-week's notice.

Part of my rationalization was that I knew I would be starting my capstone and it would be nice to have some extra time to focus on finishing strong for my college career. Plus, I could start looking for real, full-time jobs with benefits for post-graduation. Mitchell, however, did not agree. His exact words: "I never knew you to be selfish or a quitter, and I think you're being both."

I was crushed. I was angry and hurt, but mostly exhausted. It had been an emotional roller coaster deciding what to do, while still managing classes and dealing with his erratic mood swings. I was grateful we were on the phone when he made his comment and not face-to-face. As tears streamed down my face, I longed for the Mitchell I fell in love with. The one who told me we were a team and we'd get through everything. I wanted...needed affirmation that I was making the right choice. Even if he didn't agree with the decision, I needed support, love, and encouragement. I did have doubts. I did feel like I had given up. Hearing him say he thought the same was like a jolt of electricity to my heart. Painful and shocking.

Ultimately though, it was what I needed to wake up and realize I had to make a change.

I started distancing myself. Initially, I used capstone as an excuse. It was partially true. Prepping for graduation was intense. He was no longer taking German, so we didn't have weekly sessions anymore, but he still called me, would see me between classes on campus, and we would still meet for dinner every other week or so, but I limited what I said about myself or my life. I let him talk. I listened to his stories and plans. If attention was placed on me, I redirected the conversation back to him. I learned how to close him out of my heart, out of my personal life, and out of my head.

There were no more flash forwards or discussions about *our* future together. He would talk about his upcoming study abroad course and his desire to take a semester off and travel through Europe. When I told him I had an interview for a program director position at another youth organization, he said, "Big surprise. Of course you'd stay close to home." It was three weeks until I called him again after that comment.

I'd finally give in because I wanted to hear his voice, and then instantly regret having made the call. The sweet, caring, and kind Mitch had been long gone and there were no more signs that he'd be returning anytime soon. I deleted his number from my phone. Of course I had it memorized, but it helped remind me when I'd feel the urge to call him that there was a reason I shouldn't. I'd hear a song on the radio, one of our songs, and I'd reach for my phone to call him. As I'd start to punch in the numbers, I'd get half-way through, and hit cancel. As much as the song made me smile and long to hear his voice, I knew the feeling would be extinguished the moment he answered with sarcasm, intentionally inflicted hurtful words, or just bitter indifference. The extra seconds required to dial his number gave me just enough time to hesitate and stop myself from being punched in the heart.

Lingering Doubts

There were many reasons why I was against online dating or why I resisted so much. I had already identified that body image and logistics were some of the hindering factors, but there was more to it than that. I had always resisted getting into or following the latest hype. *Harry Potter?* No thanks – at least not initially. I finally caved after being persuaded by a good friend to give it a try, but I'll tell you, I held out for a *long* time. I didn't start reading the first book until the 6th one was about to hit the stores. *Hunger Games?* Not yet! Online dating seemed to be the latest fad, and I wasn't going to be a part of the wave of those blindly grasping on to what was hot right now. Everyone was doing it – it was the "cool" thing to do, so naturally, I resisted. Besides, I had other things to deal with; too many other demands and obligations I told myself.

Obviously, this was the easy way out, the surface level reasoning for not trying it. The other reasons were murkier pieces I rarely thought about. The insecurities were easier to ignore than to actually face and overcome. Ultimately though, it all boils down to one fact and one question: *I use a wheelchair – who would pick me?* It seems ridiculous to write it so simply, but that has been the fundamental fear. I cannot control or change this one thing about me. I am intelligent. I can get a Ph.D. if I want. I am financially independent and I can make more money. I can put myself out there. I can go on dates. I can lose weight even though I'll never be a supermodel. I can be active, but not in the same ways as most people.

Once someone knows this, once they get to know me, what if it's not enough? I can't fix it, I can't improve the obvious, most impactful aspect of myself. There is no plastic surgery option or magic pill I can take. It is as permanent and attached to me as my shadow. So whoever I meet will need to accept that, to live with it, to embrace it as part of what makes me, me. Who could? Who would? Is there anyone patient enough, secure enough, carefree enough to not let this get in the way of loving me? I used to joke - you know the kind of joke that masks the truth - that in high school in order to be friends with me you had to be able to lift me, take me up and down stairs, and have a car with a big enough trunk for the chair. I didn't demand the prerequisites. It was more that if you couldn't do these things, chances were we wouldn't be able to hangout. It was just how it worked. My conversation with Dana in that car many years ago introduced me to this reality and now the impact of her words was rearing its ugly head in the form of self-doubt.

Similarly, while physical strength isn't required, it helps tremendously, and being friends with me or being in a relationship with me will always require more patience, creativity, and understanding. It also means making certain sacrifices. I can't be on the floor at rock concerts because it is too dangerous for this girl. Accessible seating at a playhouse or fancy theater is often limited. I can't park just anywhere. I need flat pavement and enough space for the van lift to extend and land. Ironically, many quaint little restaurants that everyone boasts about their amazing tapas or fabulous happy hours often only have entrances with stairs; yes, there are many places that still don't have ADA entrances, accessible seating (i.e. low tables), or accessible bathrooms. Or for a restaurant with a sunken dining room, unless you're strong enough to take me down a couple stairs, we can't go there. When I am brave enough and accompanied by someone strong enough that I trust to push, pull, lift or carry me somewhere restrictive, we can go to those fabulous, yet inaccessible happy hours. Until I reach that point with someone though, such places are absolutely off limits.

There's no climbing onto the roof to gaze at stars and no camping in the wilderness, unless there are real, accessible bathrooms available, which takes away from the escape to nature that camping affords. Granted, some of these limitations mean you just need to find a person with compatible interests. Patience and a willingness to be creative to find solutions around certain obstacles are non-negotiable in my life. But that doesn't mean that I don't love a good adventure, a long road trip, a weekend getaway to the lake, a night of bar hopping and tapas tasting.

Each time I think a conversation is going well with a guy online, it seems that it is just a matter of time until he disappears without rhyme or reason. By the second or third day of silence all my core doubts about being in a chair begin to crawl out and cover me like a blanket. Smothering and hot. Restrictive and suffocating. These are the moments when I sing the song "Let It Be". Over and over. Despite the mantra and the repetitive reminders, there is always a part of me that can't help but wonder if they've been turned off because of the chair. Had they even gotten to the point of understanding the extra effort of choosing a girl in a chair? Or did they judge and leave simply because I am in a chair, plain and simple?

Perhaps initially it was something they were okay with accepting. Or maybe they found me attractive and interesting at first, but after really thinking through what a relationship would be like, what changes or accommodations they would have to make to be with me, they lose interest. It's not worth all the hassle. Maybe that's when they decide to hold out until they find someone else - someone who is simpler, someone for whom you don't have to think about accessible entrances and bathrooms and campsites.

How do you stop the encircling doubts that won't let up? Where do you turn for some reprieve? At some point there has to be some space for a deep breath, for recollecting, and centering. For taking a moment and remembering exactly who I am. I am an amazing woman full of talent, knowledge, and desire. I desire and I am desirable for more reasons than a chair. The chair only adds to my complexity, and complexity is not necessarily a bad thing. At least I try to believe so.

Steamy Showers

I am grateful for each relationship I have had, even the tough ones. Each one has taught me about myself, about my limits, needs, and desires. I began to truly see how beautiful and sensual I could be while I was in a short relationship near the end of my college career, a few months after officially closing the door on Mitchell. I became more confident and could recognize more of my assets when I was with him. Not only did he love my long hair, he appreciated the small mole below my mouth and he thought my chest was out of this world. While I had come to appreciate my chest and take advantage of low-cut tops to accentuate the 'triangle of awesomness', he provided true affirmation.

He was the first one to join me in the shower. Prior to him, if a guy saw me fully naked, it was in the darkness of night with bed covers nearby. He liked watching me though – in full light. I had never before felt comfortable completely undressed...visible....vulnerable. I came to relish those moments. My dorm room had a private bathroom which made it incredibly easy for us to have privacy. His eyes never wavered from me as I transferred from my chair to the shower bench which was placed inside the bathtub.

A smile would spread across his face as I lowered the straps on my bra and reached behind me to unhook the band. He insisted on simply watching until all clothes were tossed aside. Other than an occasional, "Mmm" that would escape his lips, the room would be silent until I started the water.

At this point, I would be facing the shower head, but I could feel his eyes on me. While letting the water get to the perfect temperature, I could hear him finally start to undress himself. Zzzzzt. I knew his pants were almost off. To tease him, I'd pull the shower curtain all the way to the wall as I switched from tub to shower mode. He often started by just standing adjacent to the tub, his feet still firmly on the tile floor, pulling the curtain ever so slightly to peer inside. His hand would graze up and down my back, around my neck, and down toward my chest. Finally, he'd step inside. There was just enough room for him to kneel behind the bench I was sitting on.

As I'd lather shampoo in my hair, he'd run both of his hands along each arm from the elbows upward to my shoulders or run his hands around my waist. He loved using my bathing puff to wash my back. Afterwards, he'd tell me to turn around to face him. With the water beating down on both of us, he'd again just look at me. He'd trace the funny scar along my side by my ribs and then lean in to kiss my neck.

I had never felt sexier, more beautiful, even with ongoing uncertainties in my life, and the little hang-ups about certain aspects of my body. With him, they didn't matter. They were forgotten. While he was never officially my boyfriend, our relationship had a profound impact on how I came to view myself.

There is a level of confidence that seems can only be achieved through the eyes of a lover no matter how much I wish such confidence could resonate solely from within. Seeing how he looked at me helped me to see myself in the same light. As much as parents or girlfriends or even your best guy friends can tell you how beautiful or sexy you look, hearing it from your partner and feeling it in their kiss – there is no substitute.

When we look in the mirror, it can be difficult to see objectively what is actually in front us. The image reflected back is filtered, distorted by doubts, criticisms, and misperceptions. In this moment, when I looked deeply into my lover's eyes the reflection I saw of myself was shaped by *his* perceptions, beliefs, and desire for me. Through his eyes, I began to shift my perspective to be outside of, and free from my inner critic. I was suddenly free to recognize my own beauty, sexiness, and strength without the self-inflicted, dismissive fine print I had been quick to add over the years of drafting my narrative of self-worth. Over time I have removed the filters, one by one, that have blurred my own reflection in the mirror. It took me a long time to get to a point where the woman I see reflected in the mirror more closely matches the real version of me, the one who can be seen as, and who sees herself as sexy, confident, uniquely beautiful; me. She is coming into finer focus each and every day.

You Love Me, You Love Me Not

I have avoided writing about him. I used so many words on him during our relationship and I spent so many years trying to forget him…to move on from him, that I couldn't seem to bring myself to open up Pandora's Box again. His name was Tim, also known as the Heartbreaker, McDreamy or McBastard (borrowed from *Grey's Anatomy*), Jerky Jerk, the Teacher, Timmy Boy, and the great love of my young life.

In lieu of writing fresh words for this old wound, I have drawn inspiration from the endless journal entries that documented what was simultaneously the most exhilarating and painful relationship of my early adult life. With few exceptions, I have left the entries intact, in their most embarrassing, repetitive, and deeply personal form. I am reminded of lyrics from Anna Nalick's song "Breathe" which I can sing by heart forward and back. It was the theme song for so very long. The day I heard the song for the first time I thought I would cry out loud. Suddenly it all made so much sense, and how did she know exactly how I was feeling? I couldn't figure out how to put words together in a way that could accurately explain how everything was all jumbled up inside until I heard that song. She was awake in the middle of the night and couldn't get her brain to stop, so she sings about how she has to write it all down, get it all out on paper, even though it will expose her and make her more vulnerable. Here goes…this is my turn to get it all out on paper, to get it out of my heart and erased from the dark corners of my head by exposing it to the light.

Late Fall 2005

For Tim's birthday, I wrote up a mock interview for his future autobiography.

When did you first meet Tim?

    I officially met Tim my freshman year of college at our dorm wing meeting. It was a Sunday evening, and all I can remember was that he had a fabulous, magnetic smile, and was a very polite, nice boy.

    The first conversation I remember having with Tim was about how he could no longer sleep naked in his room, as I had a direct view of his bed from my desk when our doors were open to the hallway.

What were your first impressions of Tim?

    I thought Tim was a wonderfully kind person. After learning that he was incredibly talented musically, I began to refer to him as "My cute, musician, dork friend" as well as "The good boy next door."

    As I got to know him a little better, I felt that he had a lot of pent up sexual tension, as our conversations inevitably included references to sex and being naked or "nakedness" as he liked to refer to the topic.

What are some of your favorite memories of Tim?

    Some of my most favorite memories are from my freshman year. I had numerous computer problems, so I would spend hours at a time in Tim's room using his roommate's computer. When I wasn't working online, I would help Tim fold his laundry or I would listen to him play the keyboard. And as he uttered a slight laugh while he played, I would envision him as an old, crazy man laughing hysterically to himself as he played some beautiful composition in the attic of a Victorian house.

    I further enjoyed the countless looks of shock and simultaneous intrigue as he gazed at my posters of naked women (in actuality, they were paintings by John William Waterhouse) or read my sexually explicit lyrics and quotations I had posted on the walls.

    However, here is my all time favorite memory of Tim: It was pouring down rain and freezing cold outside as I was getting out of class and heading to my car. It was just a miserable, gross day. As I was going down the path, I passed Tim, we said our hellos, and then he was on his way. But a few seconds later, Tim reappeared in front of me, took off his jacket, wrapped it around me, patted my shoulder, and ran off. I was already drenched and the jacket didn't actually help that much, but that small gesture made all the rain and cloudiness disappear. I had a wonderful day after that.

How has Tim impacted your life?

Tim is the reason I started a journal, and kept one for all four years of college. During school, just seeing Tim in passing made my dark days brighter. I began thinking about music in new ways, wondering what Tim would think about it, or say about it, or what he would appreciate about a particular piece.

I didn't see much of Tim for my last two years of school, but a chance reunion in December of my senior year had an unbelievable impact on my life. Work, relationships, and the stress of graduating were becoming overwhelming. I was feeling betrayed and unsure about life. In the half hour I spent talking with Tim, he had found a way to give me hope. He said he had created a new religion which had one basic tenet: "Everything is good." It seemed almost too simple and too easy, but it made all the difference. Even though I couldn't see it at that moment, everything that had happened would end up shaping who I was going to become and I would be the better for it.

After that meeting, I didn't see or talk to Tim again for almost a year. I kept meaning to call, but for some reason it just didn't happen, even though I thought of him often. I finally made up my mind to call him in September (of 2005). We talked for a long while on the phone and then we spent the whole next day together. We realized as I was leaving his place, that that day was the longest amount of time we had spent together in a single setting in all four years of knowing each other. While I had known Tim before and he was still very much the Tim I knew from school, there was a part of me that felt like I was meeting someone completely new.

This new person was absolutely amazing. I had always known Tim was this smart, caring, wonderful person, but as I was getting to know him again, it hit me just how ridiculously brilliant, funny, talented, motivated, and energized he was. Seeing this person, the same age as me, living independently with a full-time job that was his life's passion moved me. I suddenly wanted to do more with my life: study for the GRE's so I could go to grad school, move out of my parent's house and into my own apartment, read more, learn, get involved with politics again, anything, everything; he gave me energy, fuel.

I could go on and on about how Tim has impacted my life, but to simplify it and sum it all up, I'll say this: Tim has made me and continues to make me want and strive to be a better person.

I remember watching Tim as he opened his present and read through my responses. He was silent at first. Then he looked up at me, with tears in his eyes and a smile on his face. He leaned in, kissed me, and thanked me for the best birthday gift he had ever received.

Reflecting Back to 2005

It was September 11th, of all days, that we hung out for the first time since graduating. We spent 12 hours together that day, starting at my house with him working on the old organ and ending at his house with a crazy, intense, amazing make out session. In between there, we literally smelled the roses in the garden, watched "Life is Beautiful," read Dr. Seuss and other books on psychology, talked on his porch as we looked out over the lake, ate a fresh tomato from the garden, and had pie with his wonderful, elderly neighbor along with a cup of hot chocolate. It was a perfect day.

The New Year - 2006

What a year it was, and somewhere in between there, I fell in love (again?) with Tim. What a whirlwind, roller coaster that has been. Aside from normal dating issues, Tim and I have had to deal with our own issues with commitment, insane opposite schedules, and oh yes, his confusion about his other dating relationships which he neglected to tell me about until a good month into our relationship. He came over last night, we laid in bed like we usually do, he read to me, he admitted that he's sort of dating his co-worker again, and then we proceed to make out, and he stays the night. In the morning, he actually doesn't have to leave at 5 or 7, and stays until about 10. Normally, Tim is not very affectionate in the morning time because usually he's getting ready to freak out again, and distance himself, but this morning is different, and we have a very intense make out session, at the end of which he apologizes again. We have talked about how he is a terrible person, we have talked about our commitment issues, we have talked about how we both like to flirt with other people. What I guess I don't get, is how he can still be dating someone else that he says he's not really physically attracted to, and why he won't choose to just love me. He is (noticeably) attracted to me. And I worry now that he won't want to spend time with me, especially while he's dating because we obviously end up messing around, and technically he ends up cheating.

I don't know. I really like Tim. He's intelligent, he's funny, he's beautiful. I love watching him sleep, I love listening to him read out loud to me, listening to him breathe…I just love him. He's already hurt me, by not telling me about dating someone else, and I'm pretty sure that wasn't the last time he will hurt me. But I feel like he's worth the pain, the constant unknowing, the constant back and forth thing. He loves me, he loves me not. As frustrating and irritating as this whole relationship with Tim is, it has also been the most exciting, the most amazing, the most comforting relationship. I am comfortable with Tim. I love the way he touches me. I love how he runs his hands through my hair, and how he strokes the side of my face, and how he holds me. I love how we lay in bed and read and talk, and hold hands. I love that we have more or less gone slow on the physical side of the relationship – mostly intense make out sessions and then falling asleep in each other's arms. A big part of me wishes we were in a serious relationship. Another big part of me knows that neither of us is really ready. Really, I just want Tim in my life all the time. I want to see him, to sleep next to him, to have him hold me. And if I could fall asleep to the sound of his voice every night until I die, I would be happy.

I don't want him to stop spending time with me because of our lack of self-control, but at the same time, it is excruciating to be around him and not be able to touch him, to love him. Bah, I have to face it that I just can't win in this situation right now. It's frustrating and maddening, and terrifying, and I'm sure slightly tragic. I keep thinking of this quote from "Felicity" where someone says that life's tragedies are meant to harden us, and our job is to never let them. It seems though that at some point, if you keep getting knocked down, you'll eventually just stay down there. I mean at some point, don't you find it easier to just stay down, instead of getting back up, especially when you know you'll just get knocked down again? And that seems so pessimistic and fatalistic, and a part of me wants to find some major optimistic way to look at it, but it's hard sometimes. I wonder if I will ever get too hardened, too hurt, to love again. I have resisted life's attempts so far to harden me, but how much more can I take, or how much more will I take?

Early Spring 2006

I cannot remember anymore what to say. Oh wait, yes I do. He's a jerk. He's an asshole. I should have known better. I did know better, I just refused to listen. Oh my God, he is a fucking ass. What the hell is wrong with me? I should have seen this coming. I did see this coming, and I chose to ignore it. I am an ass. I am a stupid ass. I was supposed to hang out with a girlfriend tonight. I should have just hung out with her. Instead, I cancelled plans, so Tim could come over and talk about his new girlfriend. Man, I made a good choice. He is an ass, and I am even more of an ass for having put up with his shit for so long. I really don't know what to think anymore. Part of me saw all this coming, but seriously, part of me was fooled by him. How could I have not been? He initiated EVERY kiss. He initiated everything. He once said to me, "Would it not be great to be married to Sheely?" and he's the first one who said "I love you." I ALWAYS let him decide what we were or what we weren't and what we did or didn't do. And maybe it's my fault for not having called him on stuff, but still, it seems he did lead me on. Or he didn't know how to communicate with me at all.

Seriously, though. What fucking nerve he has to come over here, and talk to me about her, and how he has spent all these nights cooking with her, and how he was with her family today, and some kid called him her boyfriend and everyone was fine with that. I can't believe he was saying that stuff to intentionally hurt me, which means he is just a DUMBASS when it comes to girls. I just don't get it. I really don't. It took all I had to keep my composure tonight. And to make things worse, he talks about her and things they've done, and they all relate to the primary insecurities I had about being in a relationship with him. So, it just twisted the knife even more. I told him I feared that I was not musical enough, that I thought he would go for someone who played cello or who was just more musically inclined, and that I wasn't athletic enough. And he talked to me before about playing music with her, and then he tells me tonight they went running together. What the hell?! Seriously. Like, I don't even think he realized what he was saying to me or how it was affecting me, and if he did, then he is even more of an asshole than what I'm calling him right now. And he made some comment about how things are moving really slow with them, like physically, and he likes that, and it just made me feel slutty.

And I questioned myself if I was too forward and too much of a slut for him, but then I got to thinking about it, and he did always initiate. And now I am being punished for it. What the hell is up with that? The first night we made out, he took my clothes off. I had talked about getting ready to leave, and then he took my bra off. HE DID IT. NOT ME. He kissed me first. HE MOVED FIRST, but then now he goes for the super virtuous girl. Does he even realize how that must have made me feel today? Seriously? Does he? It's all the more obvious that I just am not good enough for him. Now it's a complete rejection of me. I am not a good enough girl, and he likes this other girl far more than me. He sees her and talks to her daily. HE NEVER did that with me. I should have known. I should have seen this all. I let myself fall for him, and he broke my heart. It's like that Jewel song, "Near You Always" about how the guy can run his hands through your hair all the while your heart is delicately placed between his teeth and he finally bites down.

Late Spring 2006

I know a relationship with any guy right now is not really for the right reasons. I am not over Tim. I am still hurt by him. I am still angry with Tim. I am still hoping things may change with him. And that will all take time to get over. Ha, so I keep watching "Felicity" episodes, and I find so many random things that seem to apply to my life. One part said maybe you never really get over the hurt of breaking up or losing someone, but you just learn to live with it. Another one was about breaking up because things were too serious, or too heavy all the time, and part of me wonders if that was what happened with Tim. Us, having to deal with past relationships, job crap for both of us, figuring out what to do with our lives. Maybe we were just too serious, and Tim couldn't handle it anymore. Maybe I am just full of shit. Out of sight, out of mind. Break ups are just hard. Relationships are hard. We all just want to know why. Why did he pick her over me? Why was I not enough? Why were we even together in the first place? Letting go...

Summer 2006

I finally had the talk with Tim. I finally saw him again after that last horrible dinner we had. I had avoided him for a long while, and tonight, I finally told him how I took everything he said to me the last time we had dinner. It was a weird talk. There was lots of random small talk at first, and of course awkwardness. And then I just told him. And now it is finally over. He did apologize for hurting me, and he really didn't realize how what he was saying was actually hurting me. He told me how beautiful I was, how he liked how comfortable I was with my body and how physically, I was great. He told me how smart and amazing he thought I was, and how one day of me being in a teen center could make more people want to be there, and how great my soul was, how I could find meaning and purpose in life without religion, and how I saw good in people, how I was good, and I did that all just on my own. And then later he said that he really always saw me as an extension of what we were in college. I was the outlet, the person for him to escape chastity with, and how he felt that's what our relationship was going to be like in September; no commitment, just having fun, and not just sexually, just in general, but ultimately with no commitment. I wish he would have said that from the beginning. The one thing I didn't ask him, was why he could commit to her, but, part of me wonders if he really is committed to her. I mean, they just started dating, and who knows how long it will last with them. But, still, she has something that I obviously don't. And I'll never know what that is. I told him that we've never just been friends. Even in college, we always

82

had this crazy sexual tension between us, and I don't know how to be just friends with him, or I don't know if I can do that right now. I know half of this is my fault. I know I let myself fall for him, but he contributed too. He admitted that he doesn't like to not be liked, and he'll step up. So, whenever I started to pull away, he wouldn't let me. I know he's just a guy. I know he is like every other human. Imperfect. Flawed. But, I did love him. I do love him still. And a part of me will love him always. But, somehow, I really have to let go now. I have to let go of the past. I have to move forward. I have to move on.

Winter 2007

It's crazy to think that it's a new year. It was such an intense year. So much has happened, so much has changed since last year at this time. And of course I have been thinking a lot about Tim lately, and how last year on this day, he came over and we had an intense night. And now, he lives 300 miles away, and I am barely even a fragment in his life. He wrote a new blog and in it he talks about all the things he's been doing since moving, and he even mentions going to Tacoma several times. But, of course, I haven't seen him even once since he's moved, and it just kind of hurt how very little I am a part of his life. And I know I contributed to that too. We have talked a few times, and I thought things were okay with us, but apparently he just doesn't have time or doesn't want to make time for me. And it reminds me of that part in "Dear Exile"[2] where she says that she hates "how everything he does involves the decision that he didn't want to do it with me." It's so fitting. I miss him. I miss hearing his voice. I miss talking with him, and I miss how he always came to my place, and we hung out consistently. I miss our Sunday dinners. I miss that feeling of knowing he was just a short drive away.

I worry that I will never find someone, and that if I do, they won't be even half of the person that Tim is. The only thing that gives me hope right now is that I am finally attracted in a serious, real manner to someone else, and that I am finding numerous other guys attractive as well, and I actually think of potential relationships with them. For so long, I just wasn't even interested in anyone. I would recognize if someone was physically attractive, and I'd acknowledge it, but it would end right there. So, maybe I'm making progress.

---

[2] Liftin, Hilary, Montgomery, Kate. *Dear Exile: The True Story of Two Friends Separated (for a Year) by an Ocean.* New York: Vintage Books, 1999. Print

Summer 2007

It's clear that Tim has moved on, and that he definitely likes this new woman, and he definitely sees serious potential in her. In the middle of our conversation, on two different occasions, he hugged me, and just held me, and I did end up telling him what crazy timing he had, and how I had seriously just decided to let go and then he has to call and show up again. He apologized a lot, and even apologized for how he was when we were together. We talked more, I told him a little bit about my relationship stuff, and we had all around great conversations. Ah, but when he got up to leave, he just kept hugging me, and holding me, and he even at one point was on his knees to be at my eye level, just holding me and rubbing my back. And he smelled so good, and was so warm and tender.

AHHHHHHHHHHHHHHHHHHHH, just bah!! And at the door, we were talking about when we'd see each other again, possibly him coming up to help me move, and in the middle of talking, he leaned over and hugged me again. And the instant he closed the door, the tears swelled up, and the breathing became difficult, and it just was too much. I suppose I am getting better, because the tears only lasted about 5 minutes or so, and I was feeling better. And it occurred to me too that really, I never felt good enough or secure when I was with Tim. Never. I always had insecurities, major insecurities, and I truly never felt smart enough, energetic enough, good enough. I mean, he said amazing things to me, we had a ton in common, and it was by far the most mutual relationship I have had, intellectually and physically, but I've been much more confident in myself with other people.

AHHHHHHHH! I've become that whiny, pining, pathetic girl again, longing for a silly boy who doesn't want her back. It's ridiculous and fucking sad. Just seeing him again reminded me how wonderful he is, and how much we have in common, and how beautiful he is, and how kind and warm he is. Bah! And I'm not what he wants. I don't go salsa dancing with him, and I don't play cello, and I live in Washington. And I just know this girl is the one for him. He used the word love once when he spoke about her, and he's thought about the idea of having kids, and potentially how it would be to have kids with her! I mean, I remember him telling me that it would be great to be married to me, and when he mentioned how beautiful she was, he always said, beautiful next to me, as close as he was to me, and what not, but I think he was just saying it to be nice. It was the little things, that he didn't catch, that portrayed how he really feels. And it kills me. It makes the silly little girl inside me who grew up with those fucking fairy tales question whether I will ever find true love or some shit, or ever find someone as wonderful as Tim, or if I will ever be as happy, or truly happy without him, or if there really is someone great out there for me. Fucking shit. I hate when I become this girl, or when this girl comes out of me. This girl who is weepy eyed, and listening to all the sappy songs again, with the perfect, horrible, fitting lyrics.

Fall 2007

It's Saturday and it's 5:30 in the morning. Tim just left my first apartment for the last time. And for the first time, I really feel like I have true closure now. I am moving out tomorrow, to a new life in Seattle, and I am leaving this life behind; this section of my life book is ending, and it is ending with almost perfect symmetry. Just under two years ago I moved into my very first apartment, #261 at Madrona. I had chosen to move for two primary reasons: 1) to have full independence from the parents and 2) to build or maintain a relationship with Tim. He played a huge role in moving me in. He stayed with me the whole first night; that was the first time a guy had stayed the night with me, in my own place, where we didn't have to worry about visitation policies or parents, or anything else. And we've had a roller coaster relationship ever since. But, now, it's coming to an end, and not a bad end but a rather peaceful, semi-content end. Content in that this was the first time I haven't cried after him leaving in I don't know how long. I just feel it's fitting. He was the one to help me move in, and he is now the one to have begun the moving out process. And what makes it all the better though is that he is not actually helping me move up to Seattle, thus my Seattle life, my new Seattle home, is largely free of him. Yes, he helped a little bit with the application essays to get into grad school, but I have no associations of him up there.

Here, in my apartment, every room, every little thing can somehow connect to him. The candy dish on the cabinet in the hallway that used to hold Hersey kisses; he'd grab one and say I'll take a kiss, and then lean over to kiss me too. Or the couch, where he'd lay his head on my lap as he napped while I read. My bed. Ah, my bed. He slept in bed with me tonight, and I hardly slept. He is definitely committed to this new woman, and he was very concerned about sharing a bed, and that we would touch, which would lead to more touching (yet, he didn't want to sleep on the couch). I think we will always have this chemistry and sexual tension/attraction between us, but honestly, it was nice to sleep next to him one last time. And while I know he dreamt dreams of her, and he was so close to me, but not with me, I didn't have that horrible, unsatisfied, longing, sad, angry frustration that I would get back in the day when he would lay with me but wouldn't do anything because he was semi-dating someone else. Tonight, it was okay. We did touch a little bit in the night. First his arm, then our legs were over or under each other's at different times. He put his arm across my stomach at one point, and when he ended up moving away, he kissed me on the forehead before he did. He noticed later in the night, that I wasn't asleep, and he said it was because we had touched and it had released this hormone oxytocin or something like that, and it interacts well with estrogen. I told him it was okay, that I was fine. Really, I spent a lot of the night just listening to him breathing, thinking about our relationship, what it was, what it is now, what it will become. While I was awake, I kept singing that old 80s song "I can't make you love me", where she's spending one last night with this guy before she gives up on the relationship because while she feels immense feelings for him, they are not reciprocated and there's nothing she can do about it.

A little sad or pathetic I know, but as I kept thinking, I began to feel the closure and appreciate the symmetry of it all.

Spring 2008

I actually got a call from Tim, which was crazy, especially since I had seriously been thinking about him earlier that day. Crazy, crazy. It was nice to talk with him, and for once, I really felt free from his magnetic, black-hole personality that usually just sucks me back in. I told him about going to Boston with Matt, and he was really surprised (both that I travelled and went with a guy), and I think that just points again to the fact that Tim really has a hard time seeing me doing things like that, particularly because I use a chair, and that's not something I want in a guy.

Matt is great, but another part of my hesitation is that Matt doesn't have the flowers and candles and romantic side to him. I mean he doesn't say flowery things to me. I talked about this with my counselor and that it's a bit of a trade off, because while Matt may not say those sweet little things or compliment me, the way Tim might have, I know that Matt is genuine, he has integrity. Matt won't say he loves me and then a few days later tell me that he's just broken up with his other girlfriend. Matt only gives me a hard time about the things I actually have control over. So, when the elevator was stupid at the museum and was wasting what little time we had there, and I did feel a little bad about it, he just gave me a hard time about distracting him in bed and keeping him up late (things I can control). And even at the airport, when I asked him to help me to my gate and help me get checked in, which is something he wouldn't have to do with anyone else, he just bitched about the airline itself. With Tim, while he did always say wonderful things to me, I always felt very conscientious of being in a chair, and how long it took me to get in and out of a car. Tim would always make comments that pointed out I was in a chair, not in a bad way, but it was just always very much a present thing with him, that he saw. Matt has never been that way, and most times, he doesn't even think about it, like when he's tried to get me to go parasailing or kayaking or whatever. That difference is a big deal, and I think in most ways it's worth far, far more, than some niceties that may or may not be entirely genuine. I don't know that Matt and I will work out in the long run. He'll be in grad school for another three years and who knows if or when he'll move back here. Regardless, though, he has been a refreshing change.

Living the Compartmentalized Life: Part I

After my relationships with Mitchell in college and Tim "The Heartbreaker," I decided I couldn't take it anymore. I was done. Done with guys. Done with emotions. Done with roller coasters and uncertainties. Done with not knowing and not getting a vote. Just done. I knew I was complicated. I knew I needed to find someone better, someone more patient and willing to love me for me, but I was not wholeheartedly convinced that such a guy existed, and I knew that my heart couldn't survive someone else biting a chunk out of it. So, like Meredith from *Grey's Anatomy* who decided to take up knitting instead of dating guys, I chose a new hobby; I learned to play the piano. I was tired and exhausted. For several months, I had no sexual appetite. I didn't find a single man, real or fictional, attractive in the least. I spent my evenings with a midi keyboard and episodes of *Grey's Anatomy, Felicity, and Sex in the City.* It was simpler, safer, pain-free.

As time progressed, I put space between them and the present, of how I was used to it being, and I gave myself some room to breathe and entertain a new idea that maybe there was something better or easier out there. Without knowing it was happening, I developed a crush on a co-worker. He was cute, intelligent, and funny. We worked well together, and he made me smile. I never saw anything happening between us, primarily because I was technically his supervisor, but it was fun to entertain the idea, to daydream and consider the what-if of life. He evolved into a good friend and we shared many interests. I appreciated having someone to discuss movies with, or the latest book I was reading. He offered to proofread my grad school essays. I started to see that I could acquire some of the benefits of the role normally taken up by a boyfriend through other means. Namely these were multiple men existing in different roles in my life rather than one single perfect guy. I decided that there was an infinite possibility of combinations of different friends, all fulfilling different innate needs in my life. I was beginning to think this was ingenious.

Thus began the compartmentalization of my life. I essentially divided my relationship worlds into four, neatly defined compartments with clear boundaries and purpose. Combined, the compartments created a safe, well-rounded substitute for a traditional romantic relationship.

The Host, Companion, and Emergency Contact

He was the platonic friend that filled the role of companionship and mutual interests. On a Sunday afternoon, I'd drive to Jake's house for dinner and a movie. He'd make me a strong whiskey sour to enjoy out on the deck as he made dinner. Grilled zucchini was my favorite accompaniment to burgers or grilled chicken. Of course, pizza was always an option too, particularly for the nights I stayed longer. We would talk about work and I'd play with the dogs. After dinner, I'd curl up on the couch with the dogs laying on or around me and we'd watch a range of movies depending on our mood. *JFK* if we were up for a late night. *Elf* if we just wanted something fun and happy-go-lucky. It was a perfect weekend evening and a great way to refresh before the next work week.

Some weekends, while I was in school, I'd spend hours in Jake's den working on a paper. He'd bring me snacks, refresh my drink, or just check in. I'd take breaks to talk with him, watch a part of the Red Sox game, or get some fresh air. It was comfortable and comforting. We didn't have to entertain each other. It was nice to just have some company and to enjoy the benefits of a house; the open space, beautiful dogs, and a back yard. I hosted parties at his house. Birthdays, New Year's, 4th of July. We shared holidays and made extravagant meals for Easter, Thanksgiving, and one year, even a gourmet Christmas Eve dinner.

When I had my first car accident, I called Jake in a sobbing, freaked out mess. After deciphering through the first sentence or two, he just calmly asked, "Where are you?"

I stuttered out the cross streets, "Yee-ess—sler and emm-emm-el-k."

"I'll be right there."

Fifteen minutes later, there he was. I was talking with the officer when he arrived. He waited patiently and assured the officer he would stay with me until I was calm. I moved to the passenger seat as Jake climbed into the driver seat. He put his arm around me, rubbed my back, saying, "It's alright. This happens to everyone at some point. Now, you've gotten it out of the way. It will be okay." He asked what I wanted to do. I had been on my way to a conference, which he was going to be attending later as well. We came up with a game plan for him to drive us both there, and we'd deal with getting his car later on. He filled the role perfectly and without hesitation or doubt.

The Intellectual and Inspiring Motivator
When I needed to be pushed or challenged in my thinking, Sean stepped in. From the first days we started working together, he would ask me about my aspirations. We set up monthly lunches just to discuss my career plans and life goals.

"So, Sheely, where do you want to be in five years?"

"I would like to be in an executive director role."

"Really?" this incredulous question was a famous Sean response.

"Well, yes, I think that's feasible by then," I was thinking his response implied that such a goal was too high.

"Why do you want to be an executive director?"

I didn't really have an answer, other than it seemed like the logical path for moving upward in the organization and it had been a goal I had set many years earlier.

"You can do so much more. You need to be some place that draws on your true strength – your mind. An executive director is too limited for you. Forget being a director. Think past youth organizations. I'm going to ask you this question again next time we meet. So be ready with a new answer. Think wide open possibilities. Play to your assets and skills."

Wow. I had always thought that being an executive director or CEO would be a top accomplishment, and those around me, like family, friends, and teachers, had been truly supportive of these goals. Sean was the first person to blow the shutters wide open with his "sky's the limit" mentality and the first one to ever tell me, "No, you *need* to dream bigger."

Reflecting back, I wonder if Sean didn't have an idea for my path already formulated when he posed the question. As we continued to work together, I started helping him with some of his projects on the side, which eventually led to our ongoing business partnership. Our work together has afforded me the opportunity to be challenged intellectually and he continues to push me on my personal aspirations.

The Traveler
Eric had become my travel partner. He was my best friend in college, but we were never more than friends. In those days, we frequently took road trips up to Bellingham. These early trips are when I discovered how great it was to travel with him. He never minded driving my car and he would offer to lift me in and out of the car to save me the hassles of transferring. We could talk for hours and equally sit comfortably in silence. I first introduced him to Chelan, WA when I asked him to be my "date" for Madeline's wedding. Again, he proved to be the perfect companion – patient, supportive, and helpful during the wedding madness. He enjoyed being with me and my friends, and he never minded all the running around and

preparations that we needed to complete to help get ready for the wedding festivities. He was always standing by, engaged and ready to lend a hand without being summoned or asked. He was just always there when I needed him.

There are certain people you can travel with and certain people who will drive you mad. It can be a true barometer of a relationship, traveling together. Our personalities meshed well for traveling in that neither of us needed to have agenda-packed days. If he needed space, he would say so and go for a walk. He could sense when I wanted alone time with my girlfriends and he'd quietly step back before I would even think to ask. My friends and family loved him and welcomed him back with open arms. Chelan has become an annual tradition for us. Although we were just friends, having him by my side and being a "couple" as we interacted with my friends and their boyfriends or husbands, made vacationing with couples as a "single girl" much more fun and definitely less ostracizing.

The Lover
Compartmentalization wouldn't be complete without addressing one of the most fundamental needs of a relationship – physical contact. Enter Dean, a passionate, brilliant, commitment-free friend with benefits. We had been friends first, and then one day discovered that we shared a mutual physical attraction. We had a great routine, and for someone who loves consistency, it was perfect, predictable, and fun. Our schedules changed often, but I could count on seeing him regularly. Sometimes, I'd wake up at 5am to pick him up at the airport. We'd have a few hours to enjoy each other's company before he had to be at his meeting or I had to go to work. Other times, he'd give me a surprise call in the middle of the day saying he had an open lunch.

"Can you get away for an hour?" he'd ask slyly.

"I'll make it work!"

I'd find an excuse to run some errands and head home to enjoy a mid-day quickie with a few short minutes of being wrapped in his arms. As it was rare for us to see each other more than once or twice a week, each encounter was filled with unbridled heat and passion.

I'd wake up on a Friday morning, hop in the shower, shave, eat a quick breakfast, and do a quick clean of the house. All the while, the anticipation would build. Heaven forbid if I actually had to complete any work or studying before seeing him. All thoughts were on him. I couldn't wait to kiss him, to feel his hands on me, to try something new that I had been thinking about for days since our last go-around.

"I take it you missed me?" he'd say as I'd take over unbuttoning his shirt if he was taking too long.

Sometimes, he'd pause and look at me. "You are incredible."

I'd smile back, saying "Thank you," as I reached up to kiss him.

Some of my best nights of sleep were the times he visited before catching a red eye flight. I came to love having sex and then having a bed to myself. There was also no snoring or having to share the covers. I could sleep as late as I wanted and I could take up the whole bed. It was, for lack of a better word, perfect.

Stood Up

There is a first time for everything. I was already having second thoughts about meeting this new guy from OKC. For one, it happened very fast. He sent me a message and two days later we were planning to meet. I knew I was rushing in, but I was attracted to him. He was from Jamaica, was working in IT for a healthcare company, and had kids. I wasn't crazy about the kids part, but I felt that being a parent usually adds a level of maturity and responsibility – or rather, it seemed easier to meet a guy who was a parent than some guy who was truly a single bachelor with zero responsibilities.

I was adamant about selecting the place to meet even though I saw from his profile that it would likely be a drive for him, but I am glad I did. I chose my favorite local café, which has become a bit of a nonprofit hub. I arrived a little early to get some work done before meeting him. I ordered my Grande Earl Grey tea and a breakfast sandwich, then picked a table by the window, where I could see the entrance as well as the side street where most guests parked. I had about half an hour before he was supposed to arrive, so I launched into my emails.

As I plugged away on the day's list of correspondence, a colleague entered the café. We said hi, and after she ordered she came over to my table. At this point, I had about 10 minutes before he was supposed to arrive. She asked if she could sit while she waited for her order, and I scrambled in my head on what to say – I didn't want to tell her I was waiting for a date. I said, yes, but that I had a meeting in about 10 minutes. I was nervous about how I'd introduce my date if he arrived early while we were still talking. It took everything I had to focus on the conversation at hand. My mind was trying to volley between the conversation in front of me and the conversation in my head if he should walk in.

As she talked, she was animated and excited and eventually was able to sway me to the present conversation and focus on what she was telling me. In the midst of her excitement, she introduced me to a potentially huge opportunity for our business. I was ecstatic to have been at the café on that particular day at that particular time, to happen across her path and be the unexpected recipient of such a great opportunity. Her order came up two minutes before 12, we wrapped up the conversation with an "I'll email you the specifics when I get back to the office," and she was on her way.

Now I could only manage to stare at my inbox for brief spurts as I kept looking outside. I saw a tan colored SUV pull up behind my van, and the guy who got out looked like it could have been my date. He looked around and even walked up by my car and then back to his. He seemed to be looking for something. I was curious if maybe he was looking for me, so I sent a text asking, "Are you here?"

No response. The guy I was watching outside went into the entrance for the main building that sits adjacent to the cafe. Five more minutes passed. As I continued to wait, staring at my laptop, glancing every other minute out the window, my mind ran through what I knew of him thus far. I began to realize the text messages he had sent previously were more clues that he was potentially not the best choice.

"Good mornin u working today boo?" was the first text I received, followed shortly afterward with, "damn, u look sexy." Next came, "why are you in a wheelchair, honey? It's OK, don't bother me, u still sexy as hell."

Let's be honest, when I'm not in a relationship with someone, not to mention having never even met them before, these comments are hardly attractive. As I sifted through the texts on my cell, I realized there was a time in my life when I would have immediately been lured in by such compliments or language, and in fact I had been in the past. I was startled I had been lured in this time. Such empty compliments generally came from the mouths of friends with benefits – those who were only interested in one thing and had the part memorized: brazen compliments and casual sexual innuendos get the girl who is looking for the attention. Part of the allure was that it was seemingly rare to find guys who were physically attracted to me during my teenage and college years. When a guy expressed interest, any interest, I would explore where it would lead, which more often than not, meant friends with benefits.

It was now 12:35. I sent one more text message, "Are you on your way?"

Again, no response. I sent a text to my friend, "I think I've been stood up." She responded with "NO WAY!" to which I replied, "It's ok, I'm working at the coffee shop and I just got a gigantic biz lead."

She wrote back, "Well, at least you're not waiting outside at night in the pouring rain."

She had a point. This scenario was phenomenally better! Insisting on meeting at the perfect location for me made my first experience of officially being stood up *much* easier. The serendipitous business connection was perfectly poised to make today well worth the effort of working from the coffee shop instead of my home office.

From that moment forward, it was easier to filter messages online. Any message that included some basic comment about me *lookin' good* or questions about wanting to hook up that night or suggestions of friends with benefits I could now very clearly say no to, ignore, or simply delete. I was proud that I was no longer drawn in. I had finally come to a point of being closer to knowing what I truly wanted and deserved, while definitely knowing what I didn't want. Now I could, with confidence, refuse to settle for less.

Even though I'm pretty clear on what I don't want, I've tried to keep an open mind without immediately dismissing guys for whatever potentially arbitrary reason I may have. When they don't fully spell out words in email messages, it drives me crazy. But I've begun to let those things slide. Part of this commitment to remain open to men I might otherwise dismiss stems from a book I read a couple years ago entitled "Marry Him."[3] The specific piece I remember from the book was a section in which the main character (a woman) decided to pay for one of the super expensive, highly customized dating services. She ends up automatically eliminating several potential mates based on height, weight, the way they spoke, a joke they made, or any other seemingly arbitrary fault she judged them to have. The dating coordinator eventually had a heart-to-heart with her about the numerical odds of finding "the perfect mate" and implored her to be more open.

Thus, I'm trying to be open, receptive to the possibility of accepting something new; but there is something to say about falling back on gut instincts. It is easy to ignore the very obvious messages for sex. It's the more subtle ones that get me. I'm still trying to figure out the right balance and course of action. When do I give my number or agree to meet? What do I need to know first? How do I communicate that I'm not one to send texts every two minutes and if you expect me to respond to yours all day long, you'll be disappointed? How do I get them to understand that when I say I'm busy, I actually am? And if I suggest a time for a phone call, that is in fact the best available time. So when you call me two hours early and I don't answer it's not OK to get frustrated when I don't jump at the call. Some get it; many do not. In all these complexities and unspoken rules, I also still need to figure out what exactly it is that I want. The Jamaican dad actually asked me this, though I didn't see the text until after he had stood me up. Maybe if I had seen it and answered it I may not have been sitting alone at the cafe.

The truth is, I don't know what I want this minute. I know down the line, I would like a relationship, more of a permanent partnership. It's hard for me to envision being married, but I don't see it as impossible. For me, online dating right now is more about finally getting out there and seeing the possibilities; slowly learning to open myself up to being in a full, dedicated, relationship. Since it is new

---

[3] Gottlieb, Lori, *Marry Him: The Case for Settling for Mr. Good Enough*

and unknown and I've never truly experienced it before, it is difficult for me to say what I want in a boyfriend or relationship. I don't really know what that means or what it will be like. I don't have a check-list of things that will get marked off when they walk in the door. For now, it's my gut that's calling the shots. I realize that my perceptions of how frequently I like to communicate or text may change over time or with the right person. I also have learned that independence is clearly a value for me as well as something I value in a prospective partner. I lead a busy, active life and I want someone who is equally busy. Someone who does not need me to be available to them every moment of the day. For that I am sure, elbow room is a non-negotiable.

I can also admit, at this point in this great experiment, that I'm going to have to baby-step into being in a relationship. I don't feel confident that I know *how to be* a girlfriend. So many relationships have been private, hidden, compartmentalized, that entering into a fully public, real, and mutual relationship is actually a bit daunting. My friends and family all know me as a single person. What happens when I have a boyfriend and he comes with me to dinner with a group of friends? How does that work? How do I do what I have always done alone, together?

As silly as this sounds, I worry about a potential mate wanting me to change the relationship status on Facebook. I have *always* listed myself as single. While I know I'm a long way off from having to deal with social media etiquette, that question about "what do I want in a relationship" has forced me to really think about what my life will look like when I am a partner, one piece of a couple, rather than a singleton. What aspects of my life will have to change? What pieces do I get to keep the same? What will I want to change to embrace someone else? What will I want to protect as solely mine? How do you learn to share when you're not in kindergarten anymore?

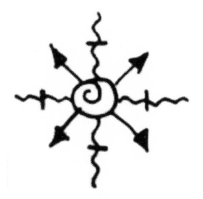

I'm a Katie Girl

There is a scene in *Sex in the City* when Carrie learns that the former love of her life is getting married, and her girlfriends talk about how the fiancé is nothing compared to Carrie. Carrie is like "Katie" – the complicated, intense, intelligent, beautiful girl from the movie *The Way We Were*. In the movie, the man Hubble chooses "the simple, plain girl" over Katie. As I was on the roller coaster with Tim, The Heartbreaker, in which he claimed to love me, but ultimately ended up wanting to date the "simple girl", I couldn't help but wonder if it was because being with me was inherently "more difficult." I challenged his assumptions, his behaviors, his words. I pushed him. Beyond that, I wasn't someone who could just wake up and go for a morning run with him or play music with him or go for a bike ride. I was complicated.

Carrie essentially follows the script from *The Way We Were* and asks Big, her former lover, why he didn't choose her. He fumbles a bit in his response, but ends up saying that *"it just got so hard."* She then places her hand along the side of his face and says "Your girl is lovely, Hubble." He says he doesn't get it, to which she replies, *"And you never did,"* and then walks away.

As she walks away in one of the few outfits I personally thought was stunning, she narrates: *"maybe some women aren't meant to be tamed. Maybe they need to run free until they find someone just as wild to run with."*

I can be quite private and reserved, generally. When I start to contemplate these complex social dynamics of being complicated, being simple, being easy or difficult, being wild or tame, I come back to the center of me, which is to be private, guarded even. I rarely share my true feelings with anyone, and in fact, when I first realize I might be genuinely attracted to someone, my modus operandi is to hide or deny such feelings. Once I finally admit it to myself and can no longer avoid the emotions knocking relentlessly, I open the door. When the feelings are finally allowed to rush in unchecked, I feel them intensely and passionately. I am certain I scared The Heartbreaker because once I admitted the feelings to myself, it wasn't long before I shared them with him. The outward signs that I saw told me that he reciprocated such feelings. He touched me, complimented me, said he loved me, and talked about what it would be like to have a family with me. He never really did though, and it took him months to actually come out and tell me, to speak the words aloud, that he only saw me as a good friend with benefits. Yes, there were some massive communication breakdowns.

I often think that perhaps I really can be too much to handle for some guys; too wild or intense in my emotions. When I feel an emotion, the expression of it is just as extreme as how intensely I feel it on the inside. The saying is true: it is all or nothing when it comes to my heart. You either love whiskey or you can't handle it at all. There is no middle ground. I don't love lightly and I love my whiskey straight.

Yes, I can have a friend with benefits. I can appreciate the company of a good friend and I can be with him sexually. However, when I truly develop feelings for him, there is no subtlety, and it becomes easy to see the best version of yourself reflected in my eyes when I look at you. The best version filled with all of that understanding and expectation of who I think you are, who I think you can be, and perhaps, just perhaps, not every man can handle that.

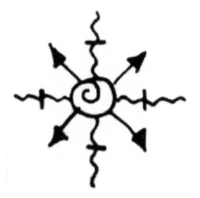

Me Before You

I thought Tim was incredible, and while he could be devastating and hurtful, I had continued to prioritize his needs over mine, to let his actions or inactions drive my emotions.

If Tim wanted to talk late into the night, I would listen, even if I really needed to sleep. If I had had a bad day, I would still ask how his day was and let him vent first, usually without ever getting around to sharing what my day had been about. I gave pieces and pieces of myself until finally, I reached the end point. I was done with all guys. I was tired of giving so much of myself only to be left hurt, distrustful, and ultimately unsatisfied. That's why the compartmentalized life was so appealing. I could keep feelings in check. I no longer allowed myself to feel deeply for anyone I was with. I created relationships that I didn't have to do so much caretaking or handholding and I could focus on my life, my goals, and my career.

I was convinced that this was better for me. Besides, I didn't have time to handle being "that girl" – the one who gave everything only to receive pieces or splinters of what she really needed and wanted. About a year ago, I happened to have lunch with a former mentor Nick, from my middle school days. We met downtown at one of my favorite lunch spots. We spent the first half hour or so reminiscing and catching up on the years that had passed. During a quiet lull in the conversation he tilted his head, looked at me, and asked if I had a boyfriend. My first reaction was a bit of frustration that this was one of the questions he would ask. After all, I had been doing so much. I completed my Master's degree, was running two businesses and consulting on the side. I was living on my own in Seattle for Pete's sake. I was accomplished! I had arrived! I was a strong, independent, successful woman. And he wanted to know if there was a guy in my life. Seriously? Why was that so important? Why was that pertinent to a conversation between old friends? Did I need one? Was I missing something? Did I not seem whole without one?

To be fair, he wasn't the only one to ask questions like this. Family and friends alike would ask the same questions when I ran into them. I used to jokingly say that that was why I went to grad school, so I could get a reprieve from the "when are you getting married?" questions and that if I started getting the questions again, I'd just go back for my doctorate.

I answered Nick by saying that I didn't really want a boyfriend. I was so busy and really enjoying everything I was doing; I simply didn't have the time or energy for one. He pushed back and asked me to explain more. I didn't really want to share that I had managed to take care of my needs by having the consistent lover, traveler, and host companion. So, I opted to share another component of the truth. I said that so often, I ended up taking care of others, and I knew I'd do the same in a relationship. I frankly didn't have the time or desire to do so. He looked me square in the eyes, paused for a moment, and proceeded to ask me a question that made me stop dead in my tracks: "Well, what about letting someone take care of you?"

Huh? What? I was stunned into silence.

I couldn't comprehend the notion for a minute. When the fog cleared and the notions became thoughts, I realized that he was right. While the various relationships I had met my needs, I never felt like anyone was really taking care of me in the same sense as a partner or boyfriend might. In college, Mitchell had started to be that person for me, and when I finally let him in close enough where he had the vantage point of being able to take care of me, he changed the rules and criticized me for needing support. Belittling me for being weak. Thinking me selfish for wanting attention. His behavior had caused me to push back, to hold at arm's length; to be wary of letting my guard down enough to have someone step in and care for me as partners do.

Of the guys in my various compartments, there was still no one to bring me chicken noodle soup when I was sick, and I was okay with that. I had become so accustomed to taking care of myself and being independent. I liked my alone time, which was reinforced by having been an only child and being an introvert. I had friends to help with certain things, sure, but ultimately, I could do everything on my own. I didn't *need* anyone anymore – not like the way I felt I had *needed* Tim or Mitch. I had convinced myself that entering into a relationship would just require more work for me. My past relationships had reinforced that belief. It is embarrassing to admit that I hadn't ever been in a relationship where my partner took equal care of me. It had always been imbalanced. To be honest, the relationships where someone did take care of me existed only in the friend category, and more often than not it was the gay best friend; never the romantic partner.

I didn't know how to answer Nick's question. I resorted to saying that I liked being independent and I didn't want to lose that. He continued to cajole saying that I could have both, that they were not mutually exclusive. His perspective was convincing and unbiased, so matter-of-fact that I began to believe in the possibility that there might be a glimmer of truth in what he was saying.

By the time I got home from lunch my mind was all a-blur with analysis, scrutiny, and evaluations. Who had taken care of me in the past, who hadn't, what was their motivation, what was the cause. It was an intriguing thought and one I had chosen to ignore for so many years that the question seemed brand new. What if I found someone and we could take care of each other? What if I let someone pamper me for once? What if I let myself truly relax, let go of having to control every detail of my days, and let someone else decide a few things for me once in a while? The thought was equally intriguing and terrifying.

I still wasn't entirely convinced, but the wheels were turning in my head. I could feel that somewhere deep down I was starting to be willing to be open to the idea. Just maybe.

A Kiss

It was a remarkably warm evening as Zach, you might remember him as the guy from my dim sum date, walked me to my car. It was our second date and we had just enjoyed a wonderful dinner (he remembered his wallet this time!). We went to one of Seattle's well known vegetarian and vegan restaurants, so we had far more options than what was afforded to us at dim sum. I enjoyed my favorite menu item – a Reuben sandwich made with Portobello mushrooms and a garden salad.

We had talked for over two hours in the restaurant, to the point where they were getting ready to close.

As we approached my car, I double-clicked the keypad to automatically open the side passenger door. As I held the switches down to operate the lift, I looked toward Zach, smiled, and said, "Thank you again for dinner. It was fun."

"You are welcome," he said while nodding, "thank you for the wonderful company."

With the lift fully on the ground, I moved past Zach, so I could back my chair onto the platform.

I pressed the switch to have the lift raise me up to be level with the side door entrance. I always appreciated the opportunity to talk with others while on the lift because I could actually be almost eye level with my standing counterpart.

I smiled, and extended my left arm out, saying, "Thank you again, let me give you a hug." Zach approached and wrapped his arms around me. It was a gentle squeeze. After a moment, he pulled back about a foot, but left one arm on my waist. Staring intently at me, he then leaned in and kissed me softly on the mouth.

While I returned his kiss, I wasn't fully expecting it and I didn't feel fully prepared. I mean we had just had dinner and I didn't have a mint or time to put on some chapstick or rather, I hadn't thought to do those things. There had been time – it didn't occur to me though.

As he kissed me again, he began to run his hands up and down my arms.

"Mmm, your skin is so soft."

I gave a soft laugh and said thank you.

He then proceeded to give me several little kisses down my left arm, saying, "Don't mind me, keep talking."

It was very sweet, and to be honest, how I always imagined a first kiss would go. While definitely not my first kiss, it was the first time I'd been kissed after a wonderful dinner filled with great conversation. Even in my past relationships, I had never kissed a guy on my lift, where I could be at eye level and have his arms wrapped around me. I hate admitting that it wasn't until I was 30 that I experienced what I would consider to be a traditional date kiss. My past experiences usually involved a massive make out session or a post friends-with-benefits, good bye kiss. This was different. It was romantic, sweet, a bit cautious or reserved; definitely not what I'm used to. It was a nice change.

My first date kiss occurred during the same week I was stood up. For a week of "first times for everything," I had no complaints. That kiss more than made up for being left alone waiting in a coffee shop.

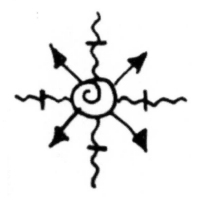

Living the Compartmentalized Life: Part II

Living a compartmentalized life meant I didn't require a boyfriend. I didn't have to open my heart up, because each compartment's relationship addressed one or more needs from sex to companionship, at least...most of the time. There were downsides to the compartments, imperfections in my plan.

The Host Moves Away
Some weekends, I would choose to stay the night at Jake's house, opting to curl up on the couch rather than drive home in the early hours of the morning. I'd wake up in the morning to the smell of coffee brewing and the dogs jumping on the couch determined to give me morning kisses. These mornings were perfect. No expectations, no schedule. Before my eyes a cup of coffee would appear with just the right amount of cream and sugar. An hour later, a plate full of the best scrambled eggs, with chives, peppers, and a dash of jalapeño, accompanied by sausage and toast on the side would be presented to me, couch-side. All before I had even unraveled myself from the pile of blankets and dogs.

Our last morning together was deeply bittersweet. I woke up to the sun shining through the blinds and the dogs panting, staring at me from inches away, waiting for their cue to join me on the couch. Jake had finally landed a job. It had been months. I was excited for him. We had celebrated a little too much the night before, but those

Manhattans had been delicious. The job was taking him cross country. It was real. He was leaving, and that was that. Of course we weren't in a 'relationship'. We were friends, and that's where the commitment ended. I wouldn't be going with him like a girlfriend might. But I had learned to rely on him like a partner; he had always been there for me, he was consistent and predictable. He made me feel anchored to a routine that I could trust when the days got hectic.

Aside from losing a best friend, I was losing a consistent companion and an emergency contact; both very dear to me. I had taken for granted the comfort of knowing he was just a phone call and a few miles away. I took for granted how easy and relaxing it was to spend time with him. It didn't take any effort. It didn't matter how crazy the week had been or what I had coming up the next week. All I had to do was drive a few miles and I could relax, escape. Now I was losing my weekend retreat.

The Intellectual Sometimes Misses the Mark

Have you ever had a bad day where all you wanted to do was go home and bitch about it over a glass of wine to your partner? The venting process is important. Releasing emotion is natural. Putting all the blame on a boss or that pesky, stubborn client is a natural tendency. Of course, there is always more to the story; I know I play a role in the situation or problem that is climbing up my spine with vigor. Simply feeling overwhelmed with the tasks at hand and needing to process them out loud is a normal way to unwind at the end of the day. Even with a clear solution or plan of action, the pressure to succeed can get the best of me at times. Sometimes, in that moment of sheer frustration or stress, when my head feels like it's going to implode, I just want to say "fuck it" and have someone, a friend, a partner, anyone, agree with me, but also tell me it will be okay. Sometimes, I just need to hear the words from someone else.

It will work out. It will get better. You can do this. I know you can.

I don't need a 10-point plan of how it's going to get better. Just saying so will be enough. This is not Sean's strength. Case in point: It was a month before the largest event I had ever been responsible for coordinating.

I was on the phone with Sean. More like processing out loud, I said, "I'm not sure how we're going to get all these sessions scheduled. We barely have enough rooms. I still don't know how many people are going to show up. I haven't heard from Luke yet about the catering."

Sean interrupted mid-stream, "I thought you said everything was coming along."

I paused for a second, feeling thrown off balance. I was definitely running through the loose ends in my head. "It is for the most part. These are just the final issues."

"Hmm, have you called Luke? Why don't you talk with Sharon about the sessions? She's done this at previous events. I thought all the sites were supposed to RSVP."

Aggravated and dismayed, I replied, "I *will*. I have it all laid out. I'm just running through the list. There's still a lot to do." Grrr. I was irritated.

"Okay," also a classic Sean response, when said in the tone that means *whatever you say, I'm moving on now.*

I sat in silence. Waiting for the *I'm sure it will be fine. You've got this.*

It never came.

Instead, he changed the subject, "Hey, we need to email Rich for a quote on that equipment."

I sighed. "Okay," the resignation clear in my dismissed tone.

The Traveler Gets a Wife. I Just Know He Will
It is only a matter of time before Eric settles down with the love of his life and I can't help but wonder how that will change the dynamic of our relationship. Even if his partner is awesome, one of several scenarios will play out.

a) She asks to join us on our annual trip to Chelan and automatically throws off the balance of our finely tuned duo by adding a third wheel dynamic.
b) Eric opts out of Chelan because he decides it is more important now to save up his vacation days for a trip with her.
c) They have children and choose a kid-friendly family destination with the obligatory visit to see Grandma in North Carolina thrown in for good measure.

Regardless of the exact scenario, the writing is on the wall. My travelling partner is not a sustainable compartment. Because eventually he will outgrow us.

The Lover's Schedule Changes
6am arrives and the alarm goes off. I prefer to wake up to music, and on this auspicious day the song of choice is "The World I Have Known" by Collective Soul. I hit snooze and lie in bed for a moment, thinking about the day. It suddenly dawns on my sleepy brain that this is Tuesday! Dean is due in town in a little while. A smile crosses my face and I feel a sudden rush of excitement. I sit up, run my fingers through my hair, and tuck strands behind my ear as I contemplate the various steps I need to take. Shower. Shave. Eat some food. Brush teeth after breakfast. Dry my hair. Prep clothes for work. I'm going to be cutting it close and want to maximize the time I have with him. Put lotion on. Cut the tags off the new negligee I just purchased from *Victoria's Secret* and put it on.

After I complete all the morning tasks, I still have about 20 minutes before I expect to receive the text message saying he's on his way. The anticipation is building. I try to squeeze in a bit of reading, but there's no use. I keep reading the same sentence as my mind repeatedly wanders back to him, to his hands, to his kiss. Ding, ding. There it is. The text I've been waiting for. As I grab the phone, I realize I'm smiling. I shake my head at how ridiculously excited I am. And then, my heart drops.

"Schedule changed. Meeting's at 8, not 10. So sorry. Can you meet at 11?"

I'm frustrated and angry and disappointed. It had been over a week since I last saw him. To say I was looking forward to seeing him would be a gross understatement. I wanted…needed…to see him.

After waiting a minute or two, I finally reply, "No, I have a mandatory staff meeting at 11." I'm grateful he can't hear my shaky, angry, disappointed voice.

"Ok, I'll be back next week."

Fine, whatever is what I want to write as I'm feeling completely pouty and whiny.

Instead, I opt for, "Sounds good."

I crawl back in bed, annoyed that a few tears well up and fall from the corner of my eyes. With a deep sigh, I re-set the alarm for nine and try to fall back asleep, wholly unsatisfied and a little heartbroken.

Grabbing a Spoon

It was a blustery winter day – one of those typical Northwest days with sunshine, rain, and even some hail mixed in, all within a few hours. I was on my way to another meeting, but needed to stop by a client's office to pick up some files. I had called ahead to ask if someone could just run the papers out to my car and save me the hassle of finding accessible parking, transferring, and going in. All in all, the process really only takes about 6 minutes with the van lift, but with the threat of a returning pocket of rain or hail it's a luxury to avoid an extra stop when possible. I was told the new assistant would be happy to do so and to just call the office when I had arrived.

So, I pulled up, put the car in park, and made the call. Within moments, I saw him approach, folder in hand. I rolled down the window.

"Hi, I'm Paul. Here you go."

I felt the words catch in my throat. For a split second, I was utterly speechless. He was gorgeous! Dark brown hair. Green eyes. Mesmerizing smile. Tall. I somehow managed to say my name and thank him for bringing the documents out to me.

"Do you need anything else?" he asked. "I just started a few days ago, but I think we'll be working together more."

Just you. You can assist me anytime! was what raced through my head.

"No, I'm good, thanks! I gotta run now, but I'll be back next week," were the actual words I managed to come up with.

It was less than a 30-second encounter, but that rush of excitement that swam over me lasted through the afternoon and evening. It had been a long time since I felt such instant attraction.

Thus, the crush began.

Over the next several months, I would discover that there was much more behind the beautiful, green eyes. He was intelligent, articulate, and thoughtful. We had mutual interests in politics, similar thoughts on religion, and equal passion for learning. After meetings, I would find myself talking with him for a half hour or longer. He learned how I liked my coffee and took over re-parking my car whenever there wasn't an open space. I would leave meetings simply beaming with joy and energy. It was rejuvenating and exhilarating to be in his presence.

Yet, we were both strictly professional. I only saw him at the office, and I couldn't figure out a) if he was single and b) how to get time with him away from work. I became obsessed with Heart's song "Alone". It's the *Glee* version I hear in my head. My favorite lines are about how being on her own used to never bother her, but then she meets this guy that changes everything and she just needs to figure out how to get him alone.

As I discussed this over dinner one night with Madeline, yes the same Madeline who would, a year later, kick-start me into online dating, she suggested I offer to talk with Paul about grad school over coffee since he had been exploring the possibility. It seemed to be appropriate enough. I was going to do it. She told me to wear a low cut, v-neck top and hoop earrings. Madeline was always thoughtful about the details.

I had a perfect opportunity coincidentally present itself. We were going to drive together to one of my presentations as he was going to be assisting me for the day. I remember the morning perfectly. It was 7:30am. I was a mixed ball of emotions. On the one hand, I was extremely anxious about the presentation I was giving – they were our biggest client and we had a lot of potential future business at stake. On the other, I was ecstatic that I would have Paul in my car, *alone*, for the first time. It was a short drive, and I only managed to hear a little about how he had been progressing on studying for the GRE's. My big successes though were exchanging phone numbers and showing that I clearly had full faith in him as I let him take my car to go back to the office while I was in the meeting.

I was thrilled, but Madeline, not so much. I hadn't actually achieved the original objective: extended alone time with Paul.

Another opportunity to be alone with Paul didn't present itself for some time. So, I continued to enjoy our conversations in the professional setting. A few months later, again at dinner, Madeline asked me where I was with Paul.

"Well, he's decided to delay grad school for a while. Nothing else has changed. We have no common friends or circles, so I don't see how I'll ever get another chance to be around him outside of work.

Madeline paused for a second and then said, "Sheely, you should ask him to happy hour. It's not a big deal or commitment. If you don't connect, then it was just a happy hour. No harm no foul. But, if it goes well, then happy hour can lead into dinner…and then, who knows…sex."

I rolled my eyes at her final conclusion.

"No, seriously. Asking someone to happy hour can still fall within the lines of a professional relationship."

I contemplated this for a moment. "Okay, but how can I bring up happy hour? We're always at work, and if not talking about work, it's topics like the 2016 elections or some great book he's reading."

"You just say it!" Madeline replied. *"Hey, we should do happy hour sometime.'* Try saying it Sheely. Practice."

I looked at her incredulously.

"Yes, say the words. Out loud. To me."

I partially rolled my eyes, shook my head, and finally said, "Hey, we should do happy hour sometime."

"Good. Say it again. *Hey, you wanna go to happy hour sometime?*"

"Hey, you wanna go to happy hour sometime?"

"Good, once more" Madeline prompted. This repeated about ten more times. I felt ridiculous.

"It's good to practice, Sheely."

As our conversations moved onto other topics, Madeline would intermittently spring in, "Hey, let's go to happy hour sometime" and give me a prompting glance to repeat her. All said and done, I must have practiced fifty times before saying goodnight.

I committed that I would ask him before our next dinner. Our dinners together were scheduled for the first Monday of each month. So I had four weeks to ask him out.

As luck would have it, a group of colleagues at his office decided to coordinate a happy hour for everyone. I managed to ask him if he was planning to attend.

"No, unfortunately, I already have other plans."

"Oh, that's too bad. Well, we should definitely plan to do another happy hour sometime. I just found a great place that has a huge whiskey selection. It's fantastic."

"Yeah, definitely. Whiskey, huh? People who drink whiskey are badass."

I was thrilled. Not only had I asked him, admittedly after having the perfect set up, he also agreed and called me badass in the same breath. I was certain that the exchange couldn't have possibly gone any better than that. I was swirling, if just a little bit, while trying to control the size of the grin that was taking up the better part of my face.

Then tragedy struck. Paul was hired by a competitor. He was leaving. For the first time in many years, I let my true feelings show ever so slightly. I sent him a text congratulating him, saying I would miss him more than I could say, and that this place would not be the same without him. At his official going away party, I gave him a card that revealed just a little bit more of my true feelings. I was definitely cautious with my heart. I followed the narrow line between friendship and love very carefully with my words, with the idea that if he just saw me as a friend, then he could read my words as such, but if he was equally attracted to me, then he could see the door was open ever so slightly.

I finally got that happy hour too. A smaller group arranged a happy hour for a couple weeks after his last day. I knew this was the opportunity. It was now or never to tell him how I felt. We were with the last wave of people to leave the bar. I offered to give him a ride home as he had taken the bus. He graciously accepted. On the drive, he shared how his new job was going. It was all I could do to actively listen. My mind was racing with how to broach the subject. I found a parking space a block down from his house. We talked for a few more minutes.

Finally, I said smiling, glancing quickly at him, and then turning my gaze toward the dash of the car, "Well, I wanted you to know that I've had the most massive crush on you since we first met."

He smiled, gave a small laugh, and said, "Well, thank you. I'm just at a place where I'm not looking for a serious relationship."

I quickly jumped in, "Oh, it's all good. I just wanted to say it. We should still do happy hour for sure though."

"Yes, definitely. I should probably go in a minute, but before I leave, I'm going to come around to the other side and give you a hug."

I know we talked for another minute or so more, but I can't remember for the life of me what was said. My heart and mind were reeling. He did come over and give me a hug. He smiled again, thanked me for driving him home, and said he'd see me soon.

That was it. On the drive home, I was remarkably okay, still exhilarated even. I was of course disappointed too, but there were no tears or "heartbreak." Ultimately, I was proud that I had put myself out there. I had finally opened myself up to the possibility of being in a real relationship. I was ready to stop living the compartmentalized life. I mean, what if he had said he felt the same way? I would definitely have had to end some of my compartmentalized relationships instantly! It would have required an immediate and drastic change. I was willing to take that leap for him.

As I continued the drive home, I thought of an early episode of *Friends* when Ross is moving into his new apartment after his first divorce. He's lamenting having to start the dating process all over again and wonders if there is only one woman out there for you. Joey says of course not – that's like saying there's only one flavor of ice cream. This is a great opportunity for you. You get to go out and try all different flavors. The world is wide open for the taking. Grab a spoon.

At the end of the episode, Ross asks Rachel, *"You know, you probably didn't know this, but back in high school I had this major crush on you...do you think...it would be okay if I asked you out sometime, maybe?"* Rachel smiles and responds, *"Yeah, maybe."* With a smile on his face and a slight bounce in his walk as he's heading out the door, Monica notices something is different, so asks what's up with him.

"I just grabbed a spoon."

Hating the Unknown
AKA: Fighting the Urge to Just Say "Fuck It"

After a few months of giving online dating a try, my patience has begun to grow weary. The constant demand to let go of the wondering, the hypothesizing, and general conundrums that have been the guys I've met so far has been exhausting. Then there is that moment when my phone rings at 4:30am and I answer groggily, "Hello?"

"Hi, I'm sorry to call so early," said the woman who I can only presume had an Indian accent. She definitely had an accent, I just couldn't put an exact region on it.

"Do you know a guy named Don Harris?"

Forcing my 4:30am brain to process the question and form a response, "Uh...sort of."

"Oh, well I'm his girlfriend. Did you two ever meet?"

"No, we didn't."

"Okay, I just found out he's been cheating on me."

What do you say to this? I would like to think that even my fully awake brain would have struggled with a response.

"Sorry. I told him I wasn't interested in meeting," was all I managed.

"Ok. Thank you. Sorry to have called so early." Click.

I set the phone down and went back to sleep. When I finally woke up at the reasonable hour of 8am, I paused. Had that conversation actually happened or had I dreamt it? I checked my phone log, and sure enough, it had.

Seriously? I thought to myself.

Then there's the guy who seemed to be brilliant. We shared an interest in writing, sci-fi, politics, cooking, swimming, and more. He's a wonderful writer. He's funny. He's encouraging of my goals and dreams. He writes me daily. After a month passed, I finally took another of many deep breaths in this crazy experiment and crossed the invisible line of the unmentionable: I asked him if he was interested in meeting and exploring something more than friendship.

He wrote back almost immediately saying, "Yes, I too think exploring something more than friendship is a natural course to follow. Now that we have that out of the way, the next steps should be easy for us to figure out."

We emailed a few more times, and then as the weekend approached I offered some potential times and locations to meet.

Silence. He completely avoided the subject in his next response. I mean, he didn't even remotely acknowledge that I suggested some meeting options. Did he receive that email you ask? I wondered the same thing, and yes, yes he did. He responded to another topic within that email in full elaborate detail. He definitely got the message.

As we continued to email, I could feel the oppressive elephant in the room growing bigger and staring me down with greater intensity as each message passed through our respective inboxes.

WHAT IS UP WITH THIS GUY??

The question flashed in my head as a giant, neon, spinning sign every time I found a new message from him just waiting for me, but knowing full well that it omitted the single, most important step of exploring a real relationship. I certainly wasn't about to bring up the subject of meeting again unless he did, thus the unanswered question remained. Lurking in the corner, ignored and left to wither away.

In college, my friends will attest that I very much liked to use the F word. As I've matured, I limit my swearing to those moments, in which a colorful metaphor is the only phrasing that will properly convey the emotion of a situation. However, there is a Sublime song, in which I used to think the lyrics went something to the effect of "fuck it, fight it" because it doesn't matter. The actual lyrics are a bit different, but I definitely adopted the use of "fuck it," when I was frustrated and just wanted to be done with something. The moment when it felt like it didn't matter what I did, the result would still be out of my control; those were the perfect cathartic moments. Fuck it.

In college, this was usually reserved for that one class where I knew after a certain point, no amount of studying was going to get me the score I wanted on the final. *Fuck it. I'm going to bed.*

At work, it was those moments when I knew no matter what facts, evidence, or case I made, my boss was going to do her own thing regardless of the outcome and as if she had never asked for my counsel. So I'd think to myself, *Fuck it. Let her do what she's going to do. She'll have to deal with the consequences.*

With online dating, I'm now left to wonder, *Is this how it's going to be? Guys who cheat and guys who don't want to meet? Seriously? Is this what I have to look forward to?*

Maybe I should truly re-consider the compartmentalized life again. It certainly has its perks. It's easier. Predictable. Organized. I can control 95% of it. I know how to navigate it. I know the down sides and I can prepare for them. So fuck it, I can go back to what's easier, simpler.

After all, I *hate* not knowing. I *hate* wondering and second-guessing myself. I *hate* it. As work picks up and I enter my busy season, how do I keep up with all the bull shit? I don't have room, nor am I willing to make room for high maintenance situations like online dating where I am bombarded by cheaters and avoiders, booty callers and deadbeats who can't keep a date.

Even the positive experiences of dating thus far have had their issues. Zach, my Dim Sum Date came over for dinner on two different occasions. The second night, we found ourselves sitting on the couch, watching a movie. After an hour of barely focusing on the film because I was wondering if and when he'd finally take my hand or put his arm around me, we finally began making out.

Then the awkward moments of "getting to know you" arrived.

"Is this okay?" "Would you be comfortable with me taking your shirt off?" "Tell me what to do. How can I help?"

While I appreciated the respectful nature of this dialogue and the fun you have with being with someone new, when living the compartmentalized life, my lover Dean no longer had to ask such questions. It was comfortable and he knew exactly what I liked and how to please me. We had been past the awkward, learning phase for a long time. Thus, I was *always* satisfied after seeing him.

This time....not so much. I know logically that these things take time, and I would be disingenuous if I said I didn't enjoy my time with Zach at all. It was fun. He was a great kisser too. I just didn't see myself wanting to go much further with him and at times I found myself comparing this experience to my times with Dean. Bad, I know, but it's true.

I have come to view the compartmentalized life as an addiction, a way of life that will be hard to live without. A routine that will take extra effort in undoing and doing differently. Dean absolutely gave me the fix I needed and wanted. Yes, there were the downsides, the crashes and emotional hangovers. The others who played roles in the compartmentalized life equally fulfilled very specific needs, and better than drugs, the downsides really only happened occasionally.

I know this isn't sustainable. I know that in the long run, I want a full life, but man, when trying to run a business, consulting work on the side, and writing your first book, there is absolutely something to be said about having designated guys for designated purposes that all fit neatly within my cramped Outlook calendar! Searching for a partner to be in a serious, real relationship with is *exhausting*. It would be so much less stressful and less tiring to just stop, to just be done.

I'm trying not to throw in the towel on dating. I know that in the grand scheme of things, I've only been doing this dating thing for a couple of months. It takes time, certainly. But damn. It is hard to resist the temptation. Old habits die hard. Particularly when said habits worked so well.

Never Too Late to Hear

I've been told this more than I remember it myself, that when I was adopted, my mom flew to India to get me and bring me back to the U.S. The story is that it took me quite some time before I felt comfortable enough to hug my mom or put my arms around her. Though the minute she directed her attention to any other kid in the orphanage, giant crocodile tears would start streaming down my cheeks. I may not have been ready to show affection, but it was clear, she was mine.

With my dad, it was different. The instant I saw him, it was love. I immediately put my arms around him and called him my "Appa", meaning "dad" in my native dialect from Karnataka. There was no trial run, doubt, or hesitation. I loved my dad.

This thought flashed through my mind as I sat next to Appa on the porch of the lake house. It was one of those perfect summer days in Yakima. Not too hot, and not too windy. Between the handmade, rock columns of the slate-lined porch, I gazed out at the lake. In actuality, it was the size of a pond. Appa had it built so he could fish for trout anytime he wanted to and peer out from the kitchen to watch the fish feeding at twilight. He had designed and built the lake house on the upper portion of the property. West, north, and south of the house were apple orchards, pastures, and even some horse trails. He had been farming for over 30 years, and it was possible, this would be the last summer at the ranch. As much as we all loved this property and the details and thoughtfulness of the architecture, managing the land was no easy task - it took a tremendous amount of effort to maintain, and age was catching up with him.

Knowing that our days to take advantage of such exquisite views were numbered, I found myself ever more appreciative of my dad's work at the ranch and of our time together. It didn't matter so much what we talked about – just that we were together. The conversation on this particular day ended up touching me deeply. After bringing out a small plate of green olives, white cheddar cheese slices, and pickled asparagus, he re-filled my wine glass with a Viognier blend and sat down.

"Did you see the Ms. Wheelchair Washington pageant or any pictures of her?" he asked. "I know you don't usually watch that stuff, but I saw her on the news."

I turned my gaze from the lake to him and shook my head no.

"Yeah, I didn't think so, but when I saw her, I thought to myself, 'She has nothing on Sheely.' You would be a knockout. It wouldn't even be a competition. I know beauty contests aren't your thing and that's good for all the others," he said as he raised his beer.

I was taken aback even as I smiled and gave a small laugh. My dad had never been one for giving me such compliments. I took a sip of wine and picked up a small piece of cheese.

"Yeah, I'm not one for putting myself out there like that," I finally replied. At this moment, I said something, I had not in a million years planned on sharing.

"Although, you know, I'm actually trying online dating right now."

A big smile crossed his face. "You are? You know my cousin Dixie has been doing that for a while. If you had told me a year ago I wouldn't have had a clue what it was and would have been worried about you."

We both laughed.

"Yeah, it has been really interesting so far," I added.

He chuckled, "Oh, how's it going? Do you have a profile up with pictures? What site are you on?"

I was surprised he even knew the term "profile". My dad is not known for being technologically savvy. Dixie must have shared quite a bit with him.

I talked about setting up the account, and how I wasn't sure what pictures to put up right away or what exactly I should say at first, particularly about using a chair.

"Well it sounds like you figured it out. Besides, you are a knockout and any guy who doesn't see that isn't worth it."

He said this so matter-of-fact that I was stunned. I couldn't even say thank you, and I don't think he realized how significant it was for me to hear these words.

He stood up. "Do you need anything? I'm going to grab another drink. I'll be right back."

"I'm good, thank you," I managed as he stepped past me.

I turned my gaze to the water and watched the slightest rustle of leaves in the aspens on the far side of the lake. It was the most gentle of breezes. Watching the Aspen leaves twinkle, I thought about why Appa's words had such an immediate, emotional effect on me. Why was I stunned?

Growing up, my relationship with mom had always been that of best friend and constant support system, and although my dad and I had our own relationship, we definitely weren't as close. Yet, his feelings or thoughts towards me were deeply, vitally important.

My mom and stepdad had always told me I was beautiful, and perhaps Appa did as well. I couldn't recall any instance of him giving such complements, and assume that if he did it was on a rare occasion, most likely when I was really young. Although mom told me regularly, I never truly believed her. I assumed it was parental bias. Yet, it always bothered me that I couldn't recall my dad saying these things, biases aside – I wanted to hear those words from him.

I split portions of my childhood weekends and vacations between my dad's place in Yakima, and my mom's house in Tacoma. I vaguely remember one incident in Yakima. It must have been when I was about ten years old. I know I wasn't in middle school yet, but I was old enough to start thinking about how I looked. My stepmom was young, nearly 20 years younger than my dad and she was athletic and fit. She exercised daily, was thin, and pretty. Originally from El Salvador, her darker features were closer in resemblance to my own, than I to my mom's fair skin, blue eyes, and blonde hair.

This is the first time I have ever articulated this out loud, but as a child I had assumed that I should have been more like my stepmom. After all, we both had brown skin and dark eyes. But there were differences that I likened to being a deficit of mine, like the fact that I didn't exercise. Sure, I swam. I crawled around as a kid, but I was chubby. As puberty hit, I gained weight and those funny thighs arrived. I certainly did *not* look like my stepmom.

To be honest, I don't know if this memory is real or conceived by the emotional turmoil of feeling an experience rather than remembering the conversation that narrated it. This particular encounter may as well have been true by how it has impacted my life. I vividly recall being at the ranch and playing in my room when my stepmom came in to talk with me. My dad was out in the orchard working. My stepmom said something to the effect that I needed to get going – go play outside, get dressed, or complete some other task. Her words implied that my dad thought I was fat, needed to lose weight, and the only way that was going to happen was if I got up and started being more active. Stop being lazy, Sheely.

I was utterly devastated and those feelings shaped my childhood, my development, and how I saw myself. Appa had never said these words to me directly. He may have never said or thought those things at all. However, I could not recall him saying I was beautiful either, and seeing how he repeatedly told my stepmom how wonderful she looked, it was clear to me, to my developing ego, that I was inadequate…unhealthy….fat.

Interrupting my recollections, Appa moved past me to sit back down, and asked, "Have you met anyone yet? Tell me about the prospects."

I loved that he was interested and that, for the first time, I felt comfortable sharing so much with him. I hadn't told too many people yet, in fact, not even mom. I shared about Zach the caffeine-free, sugar-free, vegan guy, and the guy who kept sending me incessant text messages.

"Oh boy, that one sounds way too needy. You need someone more independent."

"I agree," I said laughing.

I grabbed an anchovy stuffed olive. I had brought Appa a jar from my California road trip that past spring. We both loved anchovies and green olives – combine them together, and what's not to love?

A few moments passed by in silence as we each nibbled on snacks and sipped our drinks.

I asked Appa how the new owners were doing in the old ranch house, located on the lower portion of the property. It was the original house that he and mom had purchased decades ago, and it was the house that contained most of my childhood memories of Yakima.

"You know, I still miss that wood burning stove and the wonderful porch," I said.

My dad smiled, "Yes, it was a good home. I can still picture you in your braces, me timing you as you raced around the house. Do you remember that?"

I nodded and forced a smile as I thought to myself, *yes, of course. You always remind me about that.*

I used to have reciprocating gate braces, which allowed me to stand and walk. As a young kid, the braces were great. I was never super agile and was not strong enough to master going up and down stairs like some of the other children I was in physical therapy with, but I could get around.

I took a sip of wine, and thought it was time to confess the real story about why I stopped using braces. I had always suspected that my dad had been disappointed about my decision, but we had never talked about it. My mom knew one reason why, namely the challenges of using the restroom and getting in and out of the braces. But the first big deterrent happened in 5th grade.

"Did I ever tell you why I stopped using braces?" I asked.

Shaking his head no, "I knew it was challenging to use the restroom, but other than that, no, not really."

"Well, remember how the support straps used to fit across my abdomen and chest? When I was little, it wasn't a big deal, but by 5th grade, I had started to develop a chest, and those straps essentially served as a push up bra."

My dad cocked his head slightly. I could see him trying to recall. "Yeah, I guess I remember them having that effect."

Nodding in agreement, "Yes, well the boys in my class would snicker, giggle, and tease me about them."

"They did?" he asked incredulously. "I never knew that."

"Yeah, no one knew that. Not even mom. I tried hiding it by wearing jackets over the braces, but it didn't always work. I have never been one to share moments of true embarrassment, so I just tried to fix the problem as best I could. When the jacket wasn't working, I started emphasizing to mom how difficult the bathroom piece was getting so I wouldn't have to use the braces as often."

"Ohhh, I'm sorry. Boys can be so stupid and mean. We just don't think at that age. Well, some have that same trouble all their lives," he rolled his head back in sweet understanding and empathy.

It was nice to hear my dad say some comforting words even though it had been such a long time ago.

"Yeah, it's okay. I mean, middle school ultimately put an end to using braces anyway because of all the challenges of trying to navigate hallways. And then dealing with puberty. Mom knew that I wasn't comfortable needing someone to help me use the bathroom when I was wearing the braces, so she was fine when I decided to use my chair permanently."

"Oh, I understand. I just wish they would have worked for you longer, though."

"I know," I said nodding my head. "In retrospect, it would have been better to keep using them - health wise," I paused, "but it's all in the past now," I said with a slight sigh.

I took a sip of wine as Appa reached for another spear of pickled asparagus.

"Well, I better get a few things prepped for dinner. Do you want to stay out here or come inside? I'll just be about 15 minutes."

"Thanks, Appa, I'm fine staying out here."

"Okay, sweetheart, I'll be right back," he said as he patted me on the shoulder before heading in.

Left alone once more, I reflected on the afternoon's conversations. It was perhaps one of the most honest and forthright conversations I had ever had with Appa.

I remembered the moment I made the conscious choice to stop using my braces. I knew that by choosing to do so, I was permanently disappointing my father. I knew not by what he said directly to me, but by what he no longer said; his silence was deafening. He was always so animated and excited when I was using my braces. Even tonight talking about it on the porch brought a gleam to his eye and a bit more animation to his cadence. He loved timing me as much as I loved being timed. Each time he reminisced about these races in the past, it was a subtle reinforcement of his unspoken disappointment. I was taking the easy, no, the lazy way out. I was choosing to be less active. I was gaining more weight. It was partly my choice and partly biology; it didn't matter though. I would not be worthy of complements and the name beautiful would not apply to me. Or so I had believed based on a single occurrence that, really, who knows if it even happened for sure. But I believed it was real.

Could it be he always thought I was beautiful, but was just never any good at saying it out loud to me? Had I overestimated his disappointment in me for choosing to use only my chair?

I've had to work really hard at getting to a point where I can say I genuinely feel good about how I look, regardless of what others say or do. In some ways, hearing my dad say these words now initiated an internal affirmation of *well, yeah, of course I'm beautiful* because I now believe it for myself. It has taken time, with a few insecure stragglers still to attend to, but I have come to appreciate how I look. I don't need to be reaffirmed by others, though it is always nice to hear, especially from those you love. Perhaps it's fitting that I heard these words from Appa at a point when my self-confidence and esteem were finally at a healthier, more positive level. I may have been told in the past and didn't remember, because just maybe I wasn't able to hear them for what they were worth. My ears are finally open to hearing the sweet message from my Appa.

That day in my bedroom, I remember crying, being devastated that my dad thought I was fat. It hurt to think of him being disappointed in me for not walking. Yet, if he or my stepmom were to make a comment about my weight now, the impact wouldn't be the same as it was back then. I'm sure it would sting, but it's clear to me that finally, my self-worth is not tied up in other's opinions.

There are many aspects I like about how I look. I've worked slowly and steadily over the past year to lose weight. No diet fads or intense exercise plans, just eating smaller portions, making healthier choices, and engaging in more physical activities, including using light-weights. It has been a rewarding process to see my body change, while also feeling better and more energized. I am proud of the work I've done to look and feel better. Yet, it is amazing how powerful a few simple words from the right person, from your father, can be. It really is never too late to hear.

Jungle Curry Date

It started with a simple, "Hi, how are you?" in the chat box. I'm always a bit thrown off when someone sends an instant message out of the blue, without having sent an email message first.

I try to always respond at least once, you know, just to be polite.

"I'm doing well. How are you?"

"Doing great...Indian?" he asked.

Ah, yes, here it comes. As he was typing, I took the liberty of scoping out his profile. He was Indian, working in IT, and you guessed it, living on the eastside.

I had already become somewhat weary of the guys who messaged me that fit this profile, mainly because more often than not, they assume I can speak Hindi and that I am much more culturally Indian than what my adopted, American girl style has allowed for over the years. I suppose I actually feel self-conscious around people from India because truly, I know very little about the culture, geography, or any other aspect of India. I could qualify my love for basmati rice and Indian restaurants as being connected to my native roots, but I'd be lying. I am as American as they come.

"My name is Alak, what's yours? I love your smile. Where in India are you from? I'm actually going there in three days!"

"My name is Sheely, I was born in Bangalore, but was adopted and have lived in the U.S. since I was four."

"Nice, Sheely ki jawaani!"

"I'm sorry I don't know the reference," I typed back as my earlier intuition was amplifying and I was thinking in my head, "yep, there's that expectation for me to know all things Indian!"

"It's a Bollywood reference – Sheela ki Jawaani. It means youth of Sheela."

"Ah, gotcha. Yeah, I'm not quite on the up and up with Bollywood or really anything from India. My closest connections to India seem to be my love for basmati rice."

"Don't remind me, my mouth starts to water when I hear the word basmati."

"Haha, I know what you mean. Do you have any favorite Indian restaurants?" I asked, smiling to myself.

"Hmm, there are several good ones in Bellevue – you know, because of all the Indian coders. Haha, it's kind of a stereotype. Do many Indian coders message you here?"

I chuckled and shook my head. "Yeah, there's been a fair amount, but I think when they realize I'm more American than Indian, they lose interest. I'm definitely not your average Indian girl."

"What do you think an average Indian girl is like?" Typing pause and, "By the way, I don't have any expectations."

"Ah, fair question. One who speaks Hindi, has family in India, is super smart, works in science, engineering, or IT. I'll claim the smart piece though, but not so much in the area of science. :)"

"Well, I prefer women who are smart in areas I'm not. Complimentary in nature. Though I also consider hotness, which you definitely are!"

"Thank you." I notice I'm still smiling. It has been exactly 12 minutes, there is no way that I could actually be starting to like the short, coder boy from India. Is there?

We chatted online for a while longer, mostly about food, movies, living alone or with roommates. A little bit about family. By 10:30, I realized we'd been chatting for almost two hours.

"Well, I probably should sign off. I have an early meeting tomorrow." It was partially true, but partially, I could see myself talking with him for another two hours – too much for having just met someone.

"Oh, sure. Okay, well, I would love to see you before I leave."

"Sorry, I don't think that's going to happen. My general rule is to wait a week before meeting in person. I've had some not-so-good experiences, including being stood up."

"I understand, but man, whoever stood you up must have been crazy! OK, have a good night. I loved talking to you. Hope to talk or see you tomorrow!"

"Thanks. I might be on tomorrow, more likely Friday. Have a good trip to India if I don't catch up with you." I wrote.

"Ok, thanks. But, we will talk again before I leave."

I smiled again. Shook my head and signed out. He was persistent and even against my attempts to not think about him the next day, he kept popping into my mind.

As evening approached the next day, I finally got to a place in my work where I felt like I could sign into OKC.

Two minutes in, an IM popped up: "Hey Sheely! How are you?"

The excitement grew. So much for watching Netflix and working on projects during the evening. I was consumed with our conversation. This time, mostly about family, growing up, and other food and free time preferences.

He was pushing me more to accept his friend request on Facebook. I resisted. He found me anyway and sent me a friend request. That darn graph search made what was once a super challenging task as easy as a couple of clicks. I still held out. I was not ready to share such personal details, so I didn't accept the request.

However, as a compromise, I offered him one of my email addresses – the one I created when helping my dad manage some real estate postings online. I knew it was a bit silly, but again, I didn't want to share too much too soon and this allowed us to email and chat easier since OKC kept unexpectedly freezing during our conversation.

Then Friday's workday came and went. In the middle of the day, finding myself thinking about him, I decided to finally accept his friend request. I put him in my "semi-professional' group though to limit some of what he could see about me. Really, I just wanted to learn more about him and see more of his photos. He had some things set to public, and I had already done some research. Now I could see more of him.

At 5:30pm, I signed into email. He was online and literally five seconds later he was saying hello and asking how my day had gone.

I pointed out that I had accepted his friend request. "Oh you did? I didn't get the notification," and he proceeded to scope out more of my photos.

Thirty seconds later, "I love your profile picture…and the one with you in your car with the sunglasses. Gorgeous!"

Then suddenly, out of the blue, there was a ringing noise coming from my speakers. I didn't recognize the noise at first, and then realized he was trying to initiate video chat. With a slight flutter in my stomach, I agreed.

It was fun to see him on my screen. At first, we just typed back and forth as he couldn't get his mic to work. Seeing his smile and reactions to my comments was even more fun than the typed smiley faces or emoticons. He turned his camera around to show me his office. He was still at work finishing up a few things since he'd be taking off for India in the morning.

"You know, I'd still really like to see you in person before I leave," he implored me again.

I was tempted more than I was comfortable admitting. I hadn't eaten yet, and part of me really wanted to meet him too. The other part of me was still hesitant. Plus, it was cold outside and I was wearing my comfy apartment clothes – nothing suitable for a date.

I told him it was cold outside and I didn't feel like dressing up.

"I can see you right now. You look great. Just wear what you're wearing – besides I've seen photos of you dressed up – I know you are beautiful."

"I was just going to eat some leftovers and work on my projects tonight."

"Your leftovers will still be good tomorrow, and you'll have all weekend to work on your projects – plus I won't be here to distract you – I'll be on a plane for hours and out of the country," he rationalized.

"Well, what about the rule I made about not meeting in person until after a week? There are good reasons I have these rules in place," I argued.

"Hmm, but have you ever webcammed with anyone before you met? You've seen me now and we've talked every day."

Oh no. He had a point. Seeing him online, seeing his work badge, and knowing he was who he said he was changed the stakes completely. I felt myself caving. Now it was just a matter of deciding where to meet.

I gave him two options – Chinese food in Seattle, this Dim Sum Date would be different than the first, or Thai food in South Center.

"Let's go for Thai. How about 8 o'clock?" he proposed.

I took a deep breath. "Okay, see you there."

I knew I didn't have to change. After all, he had already seen me online, but I felt the need to dress up at least a little bit. I picked my nicer, equally warm grey Calvin Klein sweater, black pants, and my new cranberry red scarf.

I re-brushed my hair and pulled it back into a nicer ponytail, put on my boots, and headed out the door. He called me while I was just approaching the exit for the mall, and asked where exactly the restaurant was. The parking lots were appropriately full for a Friday night, but I lucked out with finding someone just pulling out of a perfectly accessible spot right across from the restaurant. The parking gods were on my side. I sent him a text saying I had just found parking and would be there in a few minutes.

"Okay, I'll come outside and meet you."

I smiled as I approached him. He was dressed casually too – dark jeans and a black jacket. I felt awkward as he walked up to me. Do we shake hands? Do we just go inside? He started to lean over just a bit.

As he hugged me, he said, "It's so good to see you."

He walked ahead of me to open the door, smiling as he did.

We had a fairly large square table, so he chose to sit to my right rather than across from me. He kept smiling and I found that I was doing the same.

"Would you like to order a drink first? You like wine right? Or would you prefer some whiskey?" Oh, he was good at this melting my heart thing.

I chuckled. "I should probably start with a glass of wine – I haven't had much to eat today, so I should start light."

We perused the menu. I asked what types of wine he liked. He was still new to the world of wine. We decided to order two different ones so he could taste both.

The waiter approached. "The lady will have the Gewurztraminer, and I'll have the Pinot Gris. Thank you."

We toasted when the wine came, took sips from our respective glasses, and then switched to sample both. He preferred the Pinot Gris, and I definitely liked the Gewurztraminer – we had made the right selections.

Picking an entrée took a bit more time. I was amazed by his attention to details. He pointed out the items with chicken for me as I was pointing out the vegetarian options for him.

I told him I was fine eating vegetarian so we could share. "You don't have to – order what you like, I can even pick around the meat."

At last, I settled on Angel Eggplant with tofu. I wanted to make sure he'd definitely be okay with sharing. He ordered the Jungle Curry.

Dinner was pleasant and I found him charming as our conversations wandered comfortably from work to family to favorite shows on Netflix. Intermittently throughout dinner, I'd catch him just watching me and smiling.

In these moments, he'd just simply say, "You are beautiful."

About halfway through dinner, he took my hand, while again telling me how he loved my smile.

I had never been on a first date like this. I was having fun, losing track of time, and I was definitely attracted. After we had completed our dinner and glasses of wine, we opted to share a glass of Chivas for dessert. Our fingers were now playfully tracing each other's. His hands were warm; his fingers long, like mine.

By a quarter to 11, the restaurant had nearly emptied. They were getting ready to close, and it was time to leave. As I followed him out the door, I admired how his jeans fit his legs. He wasn't super tall, but I liked how fit and trim his legs looked. As he held the door open for me, he said, "I don't want to leave just yet."

Across the way was another restaurant that had a bar, so I suggested that we go there for one more drink – they were open until midnight.

"Perfect."

This time, he sat across from me, but continued to hold my hand atop the table. I found it remarkable how similar our skin tones were. The pattern of lines on the palms of our hands was equally similar. We alternated tracing the life lines, as I sipped my Irish Coffee.

Shortly after midnight, it was again time to head out since the bar was closing. He reached for my right hand when we got outside and started heading to the car – I pushed with the left and it was just flat enough that I didn't really need both arms to push.

At my car, as I was operating the lift, he reached down and kissed me. Just like with Zach, the Dim Sum Date, I was caught off guard and not expecting it. I mean, I had definitely thought about kissing Alak, but having him lean down and kiss me before I was even thinking about saying goodbye was a surprise. Plus, there were still quite a few people around, and I found myself being self-conscious about such a public display. This was not my typical MO. Once on the lift and raised up to the level to enter the van, he hugged me and kissed me again. I suggested I give him a ride to his car which was parked on the other side of the mall. I was ready to get out of the super lighted parking garage with so many passersby.

He jumped in the passenger seat as I was getting ready to transfer to the driver seat. I put my legs up on the passenger side armrest and told him not to mind my legs for just a second while I moved.

"They're cute legs," he said as he put his arm over them.

Once transferred, he immediately wrapped his arms around me and started kissing me again. I was still uncomfortable that we were in the garage.

I pulled back, while saying, "Let's go over by your car." I was hoping he was parked in a less populated area, and I was correct.

I couldn't help but smile as I pulled alongside his beautiful, blue Camaro. It was so classic.

The instant the car was in park, he was back to kissing me - intensely and passionately, though at times a little sloppily. Yet, with a little direction and encouragement he was willing to follow my lead and style. I appreciated that he was so teachable.

By 1am, I knew it was time to go. He was leaving in the morning and I had a lot of work to get done over the weekend.

"Alak," I whispered.

"Yes, baby."

"It's time to say good bye."

"Are you sure?"

"Yes, you're leaving in a few hours and it's well past my bed time."

"I wish I wasn't leaving," he whispered as he held me tighter.

"I know, but we'll see each other soon." I managed.

He kissed me again, and then opened the passenger door. Looking back, he smiled, and said good night.

I was smiling the entire drive home. While in my parking garage, I saw a call come in from him before losing reception. By the time I got to my apartment, I had a text from him asking me to let him know when I made it home.

I was still settling in, when my phone rang again. It was him.

"Hello."

"Hi, I just wanted to make sure you made it home safely," he said.

"Yes, I did. Thank you for a wonderful evening."

"Oh, it was my pleasure. I'll try to talk with you before my flight takes off, but if I don't, have a nice weekend."

"Thanks, Alak. Have a wonderful time in India."

"Good night Sheely."

I couldn't believe what a fun date this had been. I mean, I genuinely had *fun*. It was a completely different experience from my first Dim Sum Date. I remember intentionally telling Zach that I wasn't much of a communicator, that I was busy, so it was okay if we didn't email or text regularly. In fact, I preferred it that way. But, with Alak, I found myself hoping we'd have a chance to talk or at least chat online once more before he left.

I woke up much earlier than normal, especially for having gone to bed just a few hours prior. I logged into email on my laptop from bed. There he was.

"Good morning, baby," he wrote within seconds.

I was beaming. We chatted for a few minutes, and truly, I caught him just in time. The shuttle was due to arrive any minute.

Part of me liked that he was leaving for three weeks. I was liking him too much too soon. I was feeling off balance with how much he was occupying my thoughts. Who knows what would have happened if he was here and I could see and talk to him every day. The prospect was a bit terrifying.

Sunday evening, Alak sent me a message through Facebook: "Arrived in India an hour ago." I was thrilled he let me know he made it safely. I wrote back telling him I was glad he made it and to have a fantastic time.

His next message put another smile on my face, "I will, but I'm already missing our time together. I hope you have a good few weeks too. I'll try to be online your time tomorrow night."

I found myself having increasing difficulty concentrating the next day. In the middle of the day, I looked at his online profile again, searched through his answers to personality questions, and looked through his Facebook timeline. The evening finally arrived. I logged in to chat and waited. He wasn't online. I tried to go about my normal evening routine – make dinner, watch the news. At last, he signed on. I heard the IM ping from the kitchen.

He asked how my day was and he shared how his trip was going so far. Then, the conversation took a bit of a turn. He told me he couldn't stop thinking about kissing me. How he wanted to do more. It was flattering to hear, but he began to get more explicit in his language. On the one hand, it was fun to have a playful, somewhat sexually explicit conversation, but on the other, I was thinking that this type of conversation was a little too familiar with its primary focus being sex. I had been down this road before in the past, but I was struggling with the evidence I had before me.

I was unable to fall asleep that night as I kept reviewing the facts and conversations we had had thus far. As I had learned with the guy who stood me up, it was pretty easy to spot the ones who were just interested in sex and no relationship. It was the more subtle guys – the ones who were equally good at conversation and romance but still ultimately interested in just one thing, that I had trouble distinguishing. Was Alak one of these guys? Had I missed something? As I reflected on our conversations, he had told me how beautiful and sexy I was on multiple occasions, yet he was also thoughtful in remembering the little details about my interests.

I continued to weigh the possibilities, and I recalled past experiences in which the guys that just wanted to be friends with benefits were also guys who never wanted to show intimacy in public. Contrary to this, Alak seemed to have no problem taking my hand and even kissing me, passionately, out in the open. That was definitely different for me. I found myself running a series of questions through my head:

What does he want? If he is in fact just interested in a physical relationship, what does that mean? If he is interested in something more, what does that mean? What is it that I'm actually attracted to in him?

I was already sensing the answer. I wanted more. I liked the idea of having a relationship, a partner, a boyfriend. I didn't want another compartment. Yet, another part of me wondered if it would be so bad to have that type of compartmentalized relationship with Alak. I mean, if he didn't want anything more, this could still be a fun way to bide my time as I continued to search for someone else who did want a full relationship.

The next morning, I slept through my alarm and ended up being 20 minutes late to a meeting. I was furious with myself. In my mind, I had no good reason to be as distracted as I had been. I hated that a boy was occupying so much of my mind, of my sleep. It was affecting my work and that was absolutely not okay. Again, I found myself contemplating just wanting to stop the whole dating thing. I can't handle the distractions, the excitement and anxiety, and constant wondering.

I talked with a friend later in the afternoon about Alak, and her response, as I could hear her smiling, was, "You're twitterpated!"

"No, I just don't know what I'm feeling or what I want or what he wants and if he doesn't want what I figure out that I want, what does that mean?"

As she chuckled, "That is the precise definition of being twitterpated, honey."

I sighed in resignation. It was true. I hated admitting it. I had to just find out where he was coming from so I could make some decisions. The endless wondering was too much to bear.

That night, I broached the subject. "What are you looking for in a relationship or what do you want...with me?"

His reply, "I don't know, haven't given it much thought." He then asked, "What impression did you get from my profile and Facebook?"

"I don't know. At first that you were looking for a partner, a girlfriend, but I'm not so sure, which is why I'm asking."

"Well, I'm not looking for anything long term or serious. Apologies if that disappoints you. I have done the long term thing before and it didn't go well."

I paused and re-read his response a couple times. There it was. Before I could respond, he asked, "What do you want?"

Again, I was faced with the question of what I was looking for. I told him I would have to think about it. He said he understood. There was a long pause, and then I finally told him that while I wasn't necessarily looking for long-term or a super commitment right now, I wanted someone to go on dates with, to share interests, hang out with friends, and yes, of course, enjoy sex with too. I didn't want a hidden relationship. He asked what I meant by "hidden" so I explained that past friends with benefits were always secret and private; no one ever knew we were together. I was tired of being hidden.

He responded, "Sure, we can do those things. You already know I have no problem kissing you in public. I'd do anything you wanted me to, anywhere, in front of anyone."

He was still emphasizing sex, and unfortunately, we weren't able to continue the conversation as his parents were calling him to join them for breakfast.

"Okay, well, have a great day," I responded.

"Thanks have a good night, honey. I may not be online tomorrow, so have a wonderful Thanksgiving and I'll talk to you on your Saturday night."

While we didn't resolve anything in our conversation, I felt much calmer, much less anxiety now that I knew where he was coming from. He was right. I was disappointed, and admittedly still a bit undecided, but strongly leaning towards ending communication with him.

I didn't need to be spending time on someone who wasn't interested in the same things as me. I want...I deserve to have more.

Epiphany

We will never know what lies before us, what tomorrow will bring, or which people will cross our paths for a moment or a lifetime. We can hope and dream, we can set goals and make plans. We can take control of our lives, live out loud, take the bull by the horns and charge head with our big ideas. We can sit quietly in the park on a sunny day and do nothing but watch. And in the end, what will be, will be. There will always be people that come in and out of our lives and we cannot always control their momentum.

The resistance to online dating had become not only about whether people would be attracted to me, or accept the chair, but whether they would also meet my requirements. There's still the desirable qualities I am searching for in addition to the non-negotiables, like sharing political and religious beliefs, interest in nonprofit causes, volunteerism and philanthropy. Will I ever find someone to fit the riddle that is all things important to me? The required and the preferred? Will any guy be willing to look past the chair, to accept that I will always have to use the chair, and choose to be with me for...forever?

One of the surprising side effects of online dating has been the bravery that has continued the momentum of the process. I have said yes to the scary, the uncertain, and the surprising, even when my immediate reactions might be to completely avoid or put off. I have said yes to things I would have otherwise said no to. Because once I made the decision to start online dating, saying no wasn't an option; saying no would impede the progress and nullify the adventure I agreed to explore. The dating process has also brought me around an unexpected corner. The corner of independence and partnership. I find myself meeting someone, and considering whether I could be with them for a long time, allow them to take care of me, carry me up stairs, or take me to bed every night. Can I wake up to this face every day and be happy?

And then it dawns on me, what if they don't *like me* like me? What if they can't see themselves with me forever? What if they don't want to wake up to me every day, with all my complexities and intricacies? What if they don't choose me? What happens then, if I choose them and they don't choose me?

I was thinking about this one night when I was trying to go to sleep, and I wondered what it would be like to find a partner who could choose to commit to a life with me and its extra challenges and occasional limitations; especially when they could choose anyone else. I mean it's one thing to marry someone and commit to love them no matter what, in sickness and in health from that point forward. But what about loving me? These insecurities have been swirling around in my head at the wee hours of the night for years, although I had never articulated them before. While I can see logically the ridiculousness of such a thought once said aloud, I continue to question whether someone out there is capable of making a vow to love me as I am, indefinitely, unconditionally, as is.

Then a thought struck me. I had experienced once before someone choosing *me* when a million other options existed, and I was chosen knowing what my imperfections were. Twenty-eight years ago, my adopted parents chose me.

My parents could have chosen any child. There were pages and pages of kids, all equally deserving, and some were absolutely perfect. Some had disabilities or limbs that were disfigured. Shortly after talking with my dad about online dating, we switched to the subject of adoption. He said it was one of the few decisions he and my mom absolutely agreed on without ever speaking a word out loud about it. They would adopt a child with a disability. End of discussion.

My dad said he had been asked by friends if he was sure he wanted to adopt a girl who couldn't walk. "Why would you do that? It's so difficult" they would ask.

His response, "Well of course we'd adopt a girl in a wheelchair! Why wouldn't you? Yeah, there are some differences, some obstacles to overcome, but so what? She is our daughter – she was from the moment we laid eyes on her."

I had this thought in the middle of the night before I ever heard my dad say the words, and it suddenly made the whole online dating process seem less scary, daunting, or futile. I had proof that there were people out there who didn't care about such things. There were people who didn't take offense or make a decision based on ability or disability, on normal or not normal, on easy versus complicated.

Now it was just a matter of finding him. Of him finding me. It didn't matter that this example was about parents choosing a child. I was now able to believe that such a choice is equally if not greater than choosing a romantic partner.

The human capacity to love is truly infinite and unconditional. Of course not everyone can do this, but I only need to find one. And truly, even if I don't find a perfect match online or anywhere else, I have experienced being chosen for exactly who I am, and for that feeling of being loved, of being chosen and cherished, I am forever grateful.

I have found the bravery to continue on this journey. I have assumed the posture of proud, confident, sexy, and vulnerable. I am amazing and wonderful, pretty and smart, scared and uncertain, hesitant and brave. And for the first time, it feels good to have them all mixed up into one ball of energy and determination. Because finally, at last, without a doubt, I know I will be successful. I know I will, *"indeed, 98 and ¾ percent guaranteed."*

About the Author

Sheely was born in Bangalore, India and was adopted in 1986 by two loving parents. Sheely currently lives in Seattle where she enjoys watching the ferries cross to Vashon Island as she works from her home office. Sheely came from a long career in nonprofit organizations working with children and teens. After 10 years in the youth development field, she decided to switch gears. With a leap of faith, Sheely jumped into entrepreneurship wholeheartedly and does not regret it one bit. While she enjoys running her own business, she has also longed to write from her heart in a creative process, the result of which is this, her first book.

Sheely is currently dating Mr. Irish Whiskey. Perhaps you'll meet him in her next book.